WEST
AFRICA

Look for these and other books in the Lucent
Exploration and Discovery series:

Antarctica
Australia and the Pacific Islands
The Himalayas

WEST AFRICA

By Stephen Currie

LUCENT BOOKS

An imprint of Thomson Gale, a part of The Thomson Corporation

Detroit • New York • San Francisco • San Diego • New Haven, Conn. • Waterville, Maine • London • Munich

Jennifer Skancke, Series Editor

© 2005 Thomson Gale, a part of The Thomson Corporation.

Thomson and Star Logo are trademarks and Gale and Lucent Books are registered trademarks used herein under license.

For more information, contact
Lucent Books
27500 Drake Rd.
Farmington Hills, MI 48331-3535
Or you can visit our Internet site at http://www.gale.com

LIBRARY OF CONGRESS CATALOGING-IN-PUBLICATION DATA

Currie, Stephen, 1960–
   West Africa / by Stephen Currie.
      p. cm. — (Exploration and discovery)
   Includes bibliographical references and index.
   ISBN 1-59018-499-8 (hardcover : alk. paper)
   1. Africa, West—Description and travel—Juvenile literature. 2. Africa, West—Discovery and exploration—Juvenile literature. I. Title. II. Series: Currie, Stephen, 1960– Exploration and discovery.
   DT472.C87 2004
   916.604—dc22
                                                                        2004015711

Printed in the United States of America

Foreword

For untold centuries people have wondered about the world outside their borders. The ancient Greeks imagined that a great land called Terra Incognita existed in the Southern Hemisphere. A thousand years later, medieval Europeans were captivated by the Venetian traveler Marco Polo's tales of the mountainous regions of central Asia and China, an exotic land he called Khanbalik. The desire to know what lies beyond what we ourselves can see is an inherent part of human nature.

But more than curiosity spurred human exploration into the unknown. Historically, most expeditions across uncharted regions were launched with practical—usually financial—goals. The discovery of a new trade route or the acquisition of new land through territorial expansion was potentially very profitable for an expedition's sponsor. In the fifteenth and sixteenth centuries, an era known as the Age of Exploration, many European nations set out for new lands and new resources to increase their own wealth, power, and prestige. For example, Portuguese navigator Ferdinand Magellan sailed along the coast of South America in search of a strait that would

allow him to bypass the stormy seas at the continent's southern tip en route to an important trading port in the East Indies. Finding a new sea passage would mean Portugal could import valuable Asian spices for a fraction of the cost of purchasing the prized goods from overland traders. In the mid–eighteenth century, England launched several expeditions from outposts in India into the Himalayas of central Asia in hopes of establishing a trading relationship with Tibet that would allow the British to expand their empire around the globe.

Though the prospect of riches and territorial gain drove most organized exploration, many individuals who led such risky enterprises gained more in terms of personal glory, honor, and sense of achievement than the expeditions gained financially. Norwegian explorer Roald Amundsen, for example, won worldwide admiration when he became the first person to reach the South Pole, though there were no riches to exploit there. The sheer triumph of Edmund Hillary's and Tenzing Norgay's first successful ascent of Mount Everest evoked a sense of awe and wonder, and a shared sense of human accomplishment, from people around the world who could only imagine the view from the summit.

Humanity has derived other more tangible benefits from journeys of exploration, geographical knowledge of the world first and foremost. When James Cook ventured to the South Pacific, for example, he charted the coastlines of many remote islands and accurately measured the distances between them. In little more than eleven years, he helped fill in a portion of the map of the world that had been empty until 1760. Thanks to expeditions such as Cook's, the geographical record of the earth is nearly complete—we know the boundaries of the oceans, the routes of the safest sea passages, the contours of the coastlines, and the heights of the earth's tallest mountains.

With each exploration, humanity gains scientific knowledge as well. Sometimes discovery is entirely unexpected: For instance, in an attempt to prevent his sailors from dying on long voyages, James Cook added plenty of fresh fruit to the shipboard diet and inadvertently discovered the cure for scurvy. Sometimes scientific investigation is a secondary purpose of exploration: For example, journeys to the high peaks of the Himalayas have yielded data on the effects of altitude on the human body. And sometimes a journey's main purpose is scientific:

Deep-diving submersibles are exploring volcanoes and hydrothermal vents twenty thousand feet below the ocean surface in search of clues to the origins of life on earth. Mars rovers are equipped with sensitive instruments to detect water and other signs of life beyond our own planet. Exploration continues as humans push the boundaries in hopes of discovering more about the world and the universe.

The Exploration and Discovery series describes humanity's efforts to go to previously uncharted regions of the world, beginning with European travels and journeys of exploration, the first voyages of discovery for which abundant documentation, charts, and records have survived. Each book examines significant expeditions and voyages, highlighting the explorers—both brave and foolhardy—who journeyed into the unknown. Exciting primary-source accounts add drama and immediacy to the text, supplemented by vivid quotations from contemporary and modern historians. Each book ends with a brief discussion of the explorers' destination as it was changed by the newcomers' arrival and as it is today. Numerous maps show the explorers' routes, and abundant photographs and illustrations allow the reader to see what adventurers might have seen on reaching their destination for the very first time.

INTRODUCTION

Lands and Peoples

Of all the world's continents, Africa ranks second in size only to Asia. Its 11.6 million square miles of land amount to one-fifth of the world's total land area, and the continent stretches close to three thousand miles both from north to south and from east to west. With such great size comes enormous diversity of landforms and ecosystems. Africa includes high mountains, low-lying swamps, arid deserts, and dense forests.

Africa's physical geography is so varied, in fact, that geographers usually divide the continent into distinct regions. Among the largest of these regions is West Africa. Roughly speaking, this part of the continent encompasses the territory that bulges into the Atlantic Ocean south of Europe and north of the equator. A more precise description might be all the land west of an imaginary line that runs from western Libya south to Cameroon. Historically, geographically, and culturally, the lands and peoples of West Africa share a number of important and distinctive traits.

Among the most significant of these characteristics is historical isolation from outsiders. For many centuries, the lands and peoples of West Africa were only dimly known to people beyond the area's boundaries. Travelers from other parts of the world rarely ventured into the area, except occasionally to visit a small strip of land along West Africa's Mediterranean coastline. Not until the 900s would people from outside the region begin visiting West Africa on a regular basis—and some parts of the area would remain unknown to all but their inhabitants until nearly a thousand years after that.

The slow pace of exploration is all the more remarkable given West Africa's geographical location. It is not isolated and remote like, say, the islands of the Pacific, which are hundreds or even thousands of miles from any other landmass. On the contrary, West Africa connects seamlessly with eastern Africa and the Middle East, and only the narrow Mediterranean Sea divides it from Europe. Yet throughout history, the people of Europe and the Middle East have usually known more about far-off lands such as China, Peru, and even the Pacific islands, than they have known about West Africa. Few other parts of the world have been so slow to give up their secrets.

Landforms and Geography

There were several reasons for the slow process of exploring West Africa. The most important of these involved climate and terrain. Much of West Africa consists of the Sahara, by far the largest desert in the world and arguably the harshest. Brutally hot during the day and often surprisingly cold at night, it is a land of windswept dunes, sharp rocks, barren mountains, and intense dryness.

The Sahara covers most of the northern two-thirds of West Africa, and it was among the first natural features encountered by would-be explorers from the north and east. Merely venturing into the Sahara was difficult and dangerous, and most who tried soon decided to turn back. The desert thus served as an effective barrier to further exploration.

The desert is not the only landform in West Africa, however. Along its southern

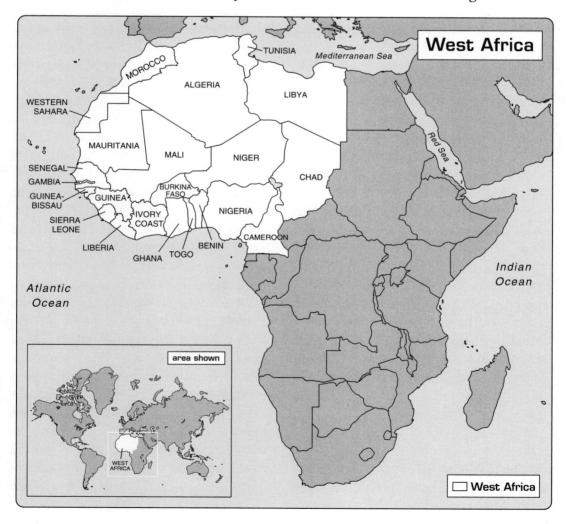

fringes, the Sahara gradually gives way to a more temperate region known as the savanna. More rain and less intense heat in this part of the continent make this area appropriate for grazing and some types of farming. Like the American Great Plains, the savanna is characterized by scrubby brush and tough, wiry grasses. (A narrower but similar strip of grassland borders the Sahara on the north as well, along the coastline where Africa meets the Mediterranean Sea.)

The savanna was the most hospitable of West Africa's climates; the trouble, for outsiders, lay in reaching it. The desert was virtually impassible, and the region that lay to the south of the savanna was not much more conducive to travel. This was West Africa's third great geographic region: the tropical forest, which runs along the coastline at the base of the Atlantic bulge. Marshes, lakes, and rivers spread out across this land; thick, tangled forests are common. The dense woods and muddy swamps of this part of West Africa forced travelers to make constant detours and hack their way through heavy vegetation. Moreover, the low wetlands were prime breeding territory for mosquitoes that spread malaria, yellow fever, and other illnesses. The tropical forest proved nearly as effective as the desert in keeping out explorers.

Knowledge and Wealth

But the barriers could not hold forever. Over many hundreds of years, explorers from various parts of the world beyond West Africa began coming to the region. The Greeks, the Romans, the Muslim merchants of the Middle East, the Portuguese sailors of the Renaissance, the English of the nineteenth century—all were attracted to the unknown region below the Mediterranean Sea. Little by little, these adventurers traveled ever deeper into West Africa and returned with valuable information about the lands and its peoples.

For some of these explorers, investigating West Africa was about gathering geographic knowledge for its own sake. The Greeks, Muslims, and English, in particular, were eager to accumulate scientific knowledge about the world, and West Africa represented one of the biggest gaps in their understanding of the earth and its geography. These explorers were eager to fill in the blank spots on maps with actual towns, rivers, mountains, and coastlines. They were in West Africa largely to collect geographical information about one of the least understood spots on the globe.

More often, however, explorers were attracted to West Africa for economic reasons. The reports of occasional travelers to the area often focused on stories of West African wealth. In particular, the empire of Mali—which reached its height during the 1300s—was believed to hold incredible riches. According to these stories, gold and other precious metals appeared throughout the imperial palaces in the Mali capital of Timbuktu (sometimes called Tombouctou to-

An evaporated oasis in the Sahara stands as a testament to the intense dryness and scorching temperatures of West Africa.

day). Generations of explorers yearned to share in the treasures of this great city.

The gold of Mali was not the only economic attraction in West Africa. Indeed, Mali was only one of several great West African empires over the years. Others, reputed to be no less wealthy in their own right, included the kingdoms of Ghana and Songhai. Even less powerful towns and governments were believed to have important trading commodities, whether in the form of gold, spices, ivory, or sometimes slaves.

Through the years, all of them beckoned to travelers eager to make their fortunes through trade.

Whether motivated by science and geography or by dreams of wealth, however, the explorers of West Africa moved slowly and cautiously. The barriers presented by climate, terrain, and disease were significant and sometimes overwhelming. Distance played a role, too; though parts of West Africa were quite close to the population centers of Europe and the Middle East, the southern and western sections of the region were hundreds of miles away from other parts of the world. And persistent rumors that West Africa was full of massive dragons and boiling oceans also kept most early explorers from venturing very far into the region.

In time, however, deep curiosity and dreams of wealth won out over the risks. Little by little, explorers traveled ever further into West Africa. They sailed along the coasts, crossed the Sahara, and made their way through the tropical forest. Along the way, they charted, measured, and took notes. The task was far from easy. Explorers suffered in the heat, grew ill from disease, and, frequently, died. But over a period of hundreds of years, building constantly on the work of those who had come before, these explorers gradually came to understand West Africa. By the late 1800s, they had successfully mapped the entire region. West Africa was unknown no more.

CHAPTER ONE

Early Tracks

The part of West Africa that adjoins the Mediterranean Sea has been known to outsiders for centuries. African seaports and settlements such as Tangier, Tripoli, and Carthage were quite familiar to the ancient Greeks and Romans, as well as to the early peoples of the Middle East. As trading vessels crisscrossed the Mediterranean, art and culture flowed back and forth across the waters. A learned Greek or Roman would have been familiar with economic and social conditions in North Africa, and the converse would have been true as well.

The earliest exploration of West Africa, therefore, concentrated on the region that lay south of the Mediterranean. Over nearly two thousand years, this effort was led by peoples such as the Phoenicians, Greeks, Romans, and Muslims of the Middle East. The work of these explorers was somewhat haphazard and did not always produce accurate information. Nevertheless, their labors were important. These early travelers and geographers were venturing into areas about which they often knew nothing. They showed bravery, determination, and spirit. Their attempts to make

sense of West Africa helped pave the way for the more systematic expeditions that were to come.

The Phoenicians

Among the first outsiders believed to have traveled south of the Mediterranean were a Middle Eastern people known as the Phoenicians, who lived in what is today Lebanon and Syria. The Phoenicians were known throughout the ancient world for their navigation and seafaring skills. By about 1250 B.C., the Phoenicians were widely recognized as the foremost sailors and traders of their region. Before long, they had settled in seaports all along the Mediterranean.

Around 600 B.C. an Egyptian pharaoh named Necho II is said to have hired a group of Phoenician sailors to circumnavigate, or sail around, the entire African continent. The sailors traveled down the Red Sea into the Indian Ocean, rounded the Cape of Good Hope at the southern tip of Africa, and crossed into the Atlantic. Then they sailed north, rounded West Africa, and returned to the Middle East through the Mediterranean. The voyage lasted almost three

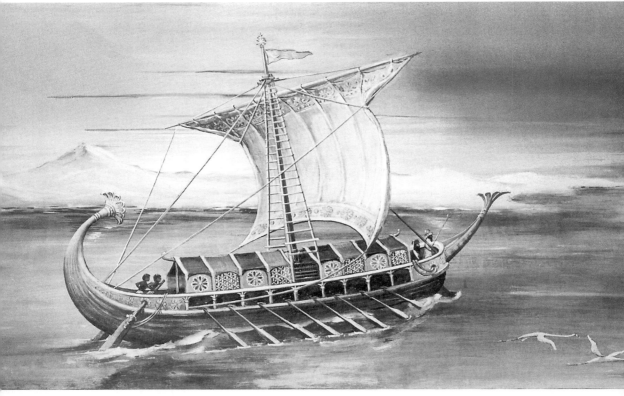

Phoenician ships like the merchant galley depicted in this illustration may have visited West Africa as early as the seventh century B.C.

full years. As far as is known, not only were these Phoenicians the first outsiders to sail along the West African coastline, they were also the first people to circumnavigate the continent.

Unfortunately, the details of the Phoenician journey are unknown today. Neither Necho nor the sailors left any direct records of the great voyage. The only remaining account of the trip is a description found in the works of Herodotus, an ancient Greek historian who lived more than a century after the expedition. And Herodotus's report is brief and lacking in detail. How many ships were sent out

is unclear; how many sailors they carried is likewise a mystery. Nor did Herodotus explain whether the voyage was undertaken for trading purposes, to gain military advantage for Egypt, or for some other reason entirely.

More to the point, Herodotus did not pass on the Phoenician explorers' descriptions of Africa and its peoples. Nowhere in his short account did he report any information gleaned from the Phoenicians about the geography of the African continent. Indeed, he saw fit to include only one discovery made by the sailors, and he relayed that to his readers in a tone of polite incredulity. "They reported things which others can believe if they want to but I cannot," Herodotus wrote, "to wit, that in sailing [westward] around Africa they had the sun on the right side."[1]

To Herodotus, the Phoenicians' observation was ludicrous. He lived his entire life in the northern hemisphere, above the equator, where the sun was always in the southern sky. Whenever he had traveled west, the sun had always been on his left. But Herodotus did not know that the reverse was true in the southern hemisphere. At the Cape of Good Hope, about as far south of the equator as Greece is north of it, the sun does appear to be in the north; the sailors would indeed have seen it on their right while sailing westward. Herodotus's confident dismissal of the report lends credence to the notion that such a voyage did take place. The idea of a northern sun could have been reported only by a traveler who had actually journeyed below the equator.

Hanno and Herodotus

Even if the Phoenician circumnavigation of Africa did not actually take place, it is certain that at least one other Phoenician expedition did visit West Africa. Around 500 B.C., a Phoenician explorer named Hanno led a large fleet west from the North African seaport of Carthage. The expedition sailed first through the Strait of Gibraltar at the western end of the Mediterranean, then headed south

along the coast of West Africa. The distance Hanno and his crew traveled is unclear, but there is general agreement that they reached Sierra Leone and may in fact have traveled to Cameroon and beyond.

Unlike the men who sailed for Necho, Hanno left a firsthand account of the things he and his fellow travelers saw and experienced. High on their list of wonders was a report of a humanlike creature that Hanno and his men called a gorilla. Hanno also described a remarkable sight he had observed somewhere along

Phoenician explorer Hanno and his crew described gorillas they spotted in West Africa as humanlike creatures.

the coast. It was, he wrote, "a country with a fragrant smoke of blazing timber . . . from which streams of fire plunged into the sea."[2] It is possible that this description referred to an active volcano, though clear evidence is lacking.

The Phoenicians were followed to West Africa by the ancient Greeks and the Romans, both of whom had a strong interest in geography. The Greek and Roman explorers, however, were more likely to travel by land than by sea. During the fifth century B.C., for instance, Herodotus—the Greek writer who questioned the Phoenicians' account of their voyage around Africa—made a journey into the northern reaches of the Sahara in present-day Libya. His description of the desert region was accurate enough to satisfy anyone that he had been where he claimed. The Libyan countryside, he wrote, was "altogether parched with sand and exceedingly dry."[3]

But not all of Herodotus's observations were accurate. Some of his information was obtained not from firsthand experience but from tales—often full of exaggeration or misunderstanding—told to him by others. The people of the southern Sahara, he assured his readers, "feed upon serpents and lizards, [along] with many other kinds of reptiles; and their speech resembles the shrieking of a bat rather than the language of men."[4] As for what lay further south, Herodotus wrote, he did not know. Whatever it was, however, he was sure it was dangerous.

The Romans and Others

The works of Herodotus became famous throughout Greece, and they remained well known even after other cultures had become dominant in the Mediterranean region. Later generations of Roman travelers and geographers complemented Herodotus's information with discoveries of their own. Around 100 B.C., for example, Roman military leader Cornelius Balbus trekked into the Sahara, looking for territory to conquer. Before returning to Rome, Balbus captured towns and cities as far south as the present-day Libyan community of Ghadames, about four hundred miles southwest of the Mediterranean port of Tripoli. And, like Hanno of Carthage, Balbus may have gone further still.

Others followed. In A.D. 42 a Roman named Suetonius Paulinius crossed the Atlas Mountains on the southern border of present-day Morocco. The first-century Roman historian Pliny the Elder wrote a description of the Sahara based partly on the eyewitness accounts of Suetonius and other African travelers. A few years later, the Egyptian astronomer Ptolemy wrote another report on the people and landforms of the desert, a report surprisingly accurate in many details. Like Pliny, Ptolemy got much of his information from people who had actually visited parts of the region rather than from personal journeys to the area.

Unfortunately, the Romans were just as prone to geographical errors as Herodotus had been. The accounts of Pliny, in particular, included plenty of misin-

Greek historian Herodutus reads from a scroll to a large audience. Herodotus traveled through the northern Sahara Desert in the fifth century B.C.

formation about the Sahara and the lands to its south. In one of his works, for instance, Pliny described a fearsome animal he called a *mantichora*. This beast, he reported, "has a triple row of teeth [and] the face and ears of a human being," as well as the body of a lion, the sting of a scorpion, and "a special appetite for human flesh."[5] A third-century Roman writer named Solinus adopted an even more fanciful view of Africa. The continent, Solinus assured his readers, teemed with dragons, ants as large as dogs, and other wonders.

But the Romans would learn little more about West Africa. Even while Solinus was writing, the Roman Empire was in decline. The Romans could no longer take the time and energy to learn about the world outside their empire; instead they had to devote their resources to protecting themselves against the raids of their neighbors. Over time, the empire grew steadily weaker, and by A.D. 500 it was no more.

With the fall of the Romans, European interest in and exploration of West Africa largely came to a stop. The people of medieval Europe had more pressing concerns than questing after geographic knowledge for its own sake. Education became a luxury, and the study of science, in particular, languished. As late as 1400, European maps and geographical treatises uncritically repeated the Roman view of the outside world—its truth and its errors alike. As far as medieval Europeans were concerned, West Africa, in particular, looked exactly as Pliny and Solinus had described it.

Arab Explorers

While Europeans remained ignorant of West African geography, however, their neighbors to the southeast were busy finding out more. These new explorers were Muslim traders from the Middle East and from the Mediterranean lands

of North Africa. These merchants were originally attracted to West Africa by stories of the wealth held by the great empires of the region. In A.D. 900, or perhaps earlier, they began to push south and west into the Sahara, hoping to reach these mighty empires and to encourage the West Africans to barter with them.

In this goal they were quite successful. By A.D. 1300, extensive trading networks linked the Sahara and the northern savannas with the Muslim countries of the Mediterranean and the Middle East. Before long, established trade routes crisscrossed the desert, each of them threading a careful path from one oasis to the next. A determined merchant could make his way from Tripoli on the Mediterranean to Kuka on Lake Chad, or from the River Niger to present-day Morocco. Traveling in large caravans for safety, Arab merchants followed these routes across the Sahara and beyond.

The journey, by all accounts, was slow and difficult. Sandstorms, heat, and sun made travel dangerous. Robbers lurked along the trail, eager to prey on the weak or those who lagged behind. Still, most of the traders returned to the Middle East with valuables such as salt, gold, and slaves. They also brought back intriguing tales about the lands and peoples of West Africa: the customs of the desert dwellers, the burning sands of the Sahara, and the glories of Timbuktu, a city said to be grand beyond imagination. Little by little, the merchants' descriptions of West Africa spread throughout

North Africa's Mediterranean coast and the Middle East.

Before long, other Arabs were visiting West Africa too. Arab diplomats and other government officials sometimes crossed the desert in order to establish political relationships with the great civilizations of West Africa. The Mali Empire, with its legendary supplies of gold, was a particular draw for many of these dignitaries. Some Muslim scholars, architects, and poets also made the trek to the Sahara and the western savanna. Un-

like the traders and the government officials, though, many of these men stayed; Mali's ruler Mansa Musa, in particular, offered money and fame to talented Muslims from other parts of the Arab world who agreed to settle in his kingdom.

Still other Arabs undertook their journeys for religious reasons. As devoted Muslims, they hoped to spread their Islamic faith throughout West Africa. In this goal they were quite successful. By about A.D. 1100 most of the desert peoples had converted to Islam, and the Mali

Geographic Misinformation

The misinformation in the works of Pliny and Solinus was quite extensive. Robin Hallett's The Penetration of Africa *presents some of the "facts" they insisted were true about African geography and peoples.*

- The Blemmyes people, who "have no heads[,] but mouths and eies [eyes] both in their breast [chest]."
- The Strapfoot people, who were unable to walk and so crawled everywhere they went.
- The Atlas Mountains, an actual physical feature, but which Pliny insisted were haunted by satyrs and other creatures so that the entire range "resoundeth with the noise of haut-boys [oboes], pipes, and fifes."
- Pegasi, the plural of *pegasus*, which in this case referred to a winged horse with horns.
- The Torrid Zone, deep inside Africa, where the sun approaches so near the Earth that the ground is "parched and fried."

The writings of Pliny the Elder are replete with misinformation about African geography and peoples.

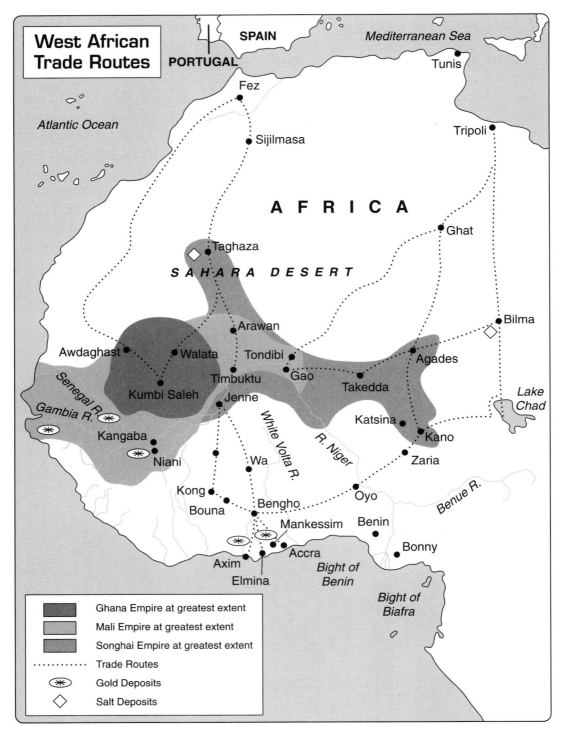

West African Trade Routes

Atlantic Ocean

SPAIN
Mediterranean Sea

PORTUGAL

Tunis

Fez

Sijilmasa

Tripoli

A F R I C A

Ghat

Taghaza

S A H A R A   D E S E R T

Bilma

Arawan

Awdaghast

Walata

Tondibi

Agades

Lake Chad

Timbuktu

Gao

Senegal R.

Kumbi Saleh

Jenne

Takedda

Gambia R.

Katsina

Kangaba

White Volta R.

R. Niger

Kano

Niani

Zaria

Wa

Benue R.

Kong

Oyo

Bouna

Bengho

Mankessim

Benin

Bonny

Accra

Axim

Bight of Benin

Elmina

Bight of Biafra

Ghana Empire at greatest extent

Mali Empire at greatest extent

Songhai Empire at greatest extent

Trade Routes

Gold Deposits

Salt Deposits

Empire, despite being located relatively far to the south, was strongly Muslim during its heyday a few hundred years later. Islam remains the dominant religion of much of West Africa, especially in the lands north of the tropical forests.

Idrisi's Map

But religion, trade, and politics were not the only reasons why Muslims traveled to West Africa. Like the Romans and the ancient Greeks, the Arab world was interested in geography for its own sake. The Muslims of the medieval period were mathematicians, navigators, and astronomers. They knew that the Earth was a sphere, with an equator dividing the world into northern and southern halves, and they could use the skies and the stars to measure the distance between two points on the Earth's surface. The Muslims of this time were eager to find out what they could about the world around them—and to record their knowledge in books and in maps.

The most famous of these medieval maps was produced by a Muslim geographer and traveler named Idrisi. Born in 1099, Idrisi was a native of Morocco in extreme northwestern Africa. He attended an Islamic university in Spain, a southern European country where Muslim influence was great; it was there that he may first have been exposed to the art of mapmaking. However, Idrisi had always been an eager traveler. During his early years, he ventured as far north as England and as far east as central Asia—

neither of them common destinations for young Muslim travelers of the time.

Soon Idrisi's reputation as a mapmaker and geographer began to spread throughout the Arab world. News of his work even reached beyond, to the kingdom of Sicily, an island off Italy's southern coast. Among Christian monarchs of medieval Europe, King Roger II of Sicily was an anomaly: Unlike most of his contemporaries, he was deeply interested in geography and the world that lay outside his own island. About 1139, Roger hired Idrisi to put together a book and a map that would together describe everything known about the geography of the Earth.

Over the next fifteen years Idrisi labored intently on his project. He talked to travelers, surveyed the writings of the explorers of the past, and learned about the landforms and coastlines of the world's continents and islands. While there is no indication that Idrisi did any further exploration on his own, some sources suggest that Idrisi and Roger sponsored several voyages of discovery. They paid travelers to investigate some parts of the world about which knowledge seemed particularly sketchy. It is possible that these destinations included West Africa, a section of the globe which Idrisi himself seems never to have visited.

Arid Wastes and Trading Centers

In 1154, after years of concentrated labor, Idrisi at last completed the project.

The finished work was enormous. The map was originally drawn on a silver tablet measuring about twelve feet long. When professional scribes created a copy, they had to use seventy sheets of paper joined together. The book that functioned as a guide to the map was first issued under the title *The Recreation for Him Who Wishes to Travel Through the Countries*. Today, however, it is better known simply as *Geography*.

A large portion of Idrisi's work deals with the African continent, and with West Africa in particular. From a modern perspective, Idrisi's representation of this region leaves a great deal to be desired. Not knowing the exact shape of the African continent, Idrisi guessed—and guessed wrong. The bulge that creates West Africa, in particular, is nowhere to be found on his map, making Africa unrecognizable to anyone looking at his images today. Similarly, Idrisi showed the East African Nile and the West African Niger as different branches of the same river, which they are not. And the map suffers from stylized shapes, misplaced mountains, and a general lack of detail that would frustrate most people today.

On the other hand, Idrisi's work often showed surprising insight into West African geography. His description of the Sahara, for example, spoke of "arid wastes where one must walk two, four, five, or twelve days before finding water."[6] Despite his belief that the Niger joined the Nile, he did put the Niger in roughly the right spot on the map. Idrisi's knowledge of sub-Saharan Africa was impressive too. The city of Kumbi Saleh in the kingdom of Ghana, he wrote, was "the most considerable, the most densely peopled and the largest trading center of the Negro countries."[7]

Idrisi's work proved influential within the Arab world. While few Muslims had the opportunity to view Idrisi's map firsthand or read a copy of his *Geography*, the people of the Middle East and the Arab-influenced regions of the Mediterranean were nevertheless familiar with Idrisi and his accomplishments. In the next few centuries, Idrisi's work inspired other Muslims to investigate the world around them. Some of these adventurers, sparked in part by Idrisi's description of Wangara's stores of gold or Ghana's "abundance of rich ornaments,"[8] headed to West Africa.

Ibn Battuta

The most famous of these explorers was a man known as Ibn Battuta, who lived from 1304 to 1368. There were some strong similarities between Ibn Battuta's life and that of Idrisi. Both men were Muslim. Both were good writers with a deep interest in knowledge and in the world around them. Both were born on Morocco's Mediterranean coastline. And both were eager and experienced travelers.

The word *traveler*, however, seems an inadequate description of Ibn Battuta. From the time he was a young man, he traveled constantly throughout the Muslim world and beyond. In addition to

The Ship of the Desert

The vehicle of choice for Arab merchants who traveled across the Sahara was the camel, sometimes known as "the ship of the desert." Camels are ideal for making the long and dangerous trek. Although they can be foul tempered, their stamina is excellent, and their ability to carry large loads is unequaled by almost any other animal, including the horse. Moreover, camels are well adapted to desert conditions. They are able to subsist on almost any kind of vegetation, their long eyelashes and small ears help protect them from sandstorms, and their feet are well designed for travel through soft sand. Best of all, camels can travel enormous distances on very little water.

It was certainly possible to cross the Sahara without the assistance of a camel, and some later explorers did exactly that. But because camels could carry so many goods with so little effort, extensive trade across the desert flourished. By 1200, dozens of camel caravans regularly wound their way through the desert. Some of the caravans included as many as one thousand camels, which between them carried tons of goods: spices, gold, and ostrich feathers bound for the north, and paper, weapons, and cloth heading south. Without the camels, trade on this scale would not have been possible.

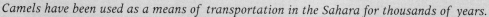

Camels have been used as a means of transportation in the Sahara for thousands of years.

Spain, Saudi Arabia, Turkey, and other places relatively near his Moroccan homeland, Ibn Battuta traveled to points as distant as China, India, and Africa's eastern coast. In all, Ibn Battuta's journeys took him at least seventy-five thousand miles; some historians believe one hundred thousand miles is a better estimate.

One of the places where Ibn Battuta spent little time, however, was West Africa. His only foray into the region came at the end of his long traveling career. In 1352, eager to investigate the great Muslim kingdom of Mali, Ibn Battuta joined a trading caravan and crossed the Sahara. He spent several months in the empire and, through observation and discussion with the people of the region, learned as much as possible about the country. Upon returning home, Ibn Battuta wrote a detailed record of his adventures, copies of which survive today.

On the whole, Ibn Battuta's reaction to West Africa and its people was mixed. He strongly disliked the trading community of Taghaza, one of the first places he saw in the Sahara, dismissing it as "a village with no attractions."[9] He also objected to the usual West African diet, which included dogs and donkeys. As a conservative Muslim, moreover, Ibn Battuta was offended by the tendency of female slaves and servants to wear no clothing at all. He was also offended by the welcoming gift he received. As an honored visitor to the kingdom, Ibn Battuta had expected government leaders to offer him fine robes, even gold, but he got only bread, fried meat, and a container of yogurt.

On the other hand, Ibn Battuta found much to admire about Mali and the rest of West Africa. He noted with approval the lack of jealousy among one Saharan

Ibn Battuta and the Sahara

Ibn Battuta's journey across the Sahara included a stay in Taghaza. His account of Taghaza and the exceptionally dry stretch of desert to its south appears in The Travels of Ibn Battuta, *vol. 4. As the excerpt makes clear, Ibn Battuta's interests were wide ranging, and he noted virtually everything he observed.*

A strange thing about [Taghaza] is that its houses and mosque are built of blocks of salt and roofed with camel skins. There are no trees, only sand in which [there] is a salt mine. . . . We spent ten days there, under strain, for the water is brackish and it is the place with the most flies. Here water is taken in for the journey which lies beyond. It is ten days' travel with no water, or only rarely. We, however, did find plentiful water in pools left by the rain. . . . Truffles are plentiful in that desert, and so are lice, so much so that people wear round their necks string necklaces containing mercury, which kills them.

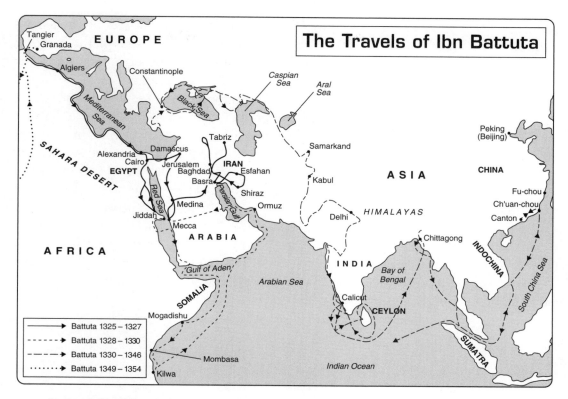

The Travels of Ibn Battuta

Battuta 1325 – 1327
Battuta 1328 – 1330
Battuta 1330 – 1346
Battuta 1349 – 1354

people, and he found the Mali Empire pleasantly free from crime. Furthermore, Ibn Battuta believed that the people of Mali were among the most fair-minded he had encountered. "Among their good practices are their avoidance of injustice," he wrote. "There is no people more averse to it, and their Sultan does not allow anyone to practice it in any measure." [10]

In most respects, Ibn Battuta's information was accurate. A stickler for truth and detail and a veteran of many earlier journeys, he was not easily impressed by stories about lands and people he had yet to experience. Unlike many of his medieval contemporaries—or Pliny and Solinus, for that matter—Ibn Battuta pre-

ferred to report only that which he had seen firsthand. "There is no road to be seen in the desert and no track," he wrote about the dunes of the Sahara, "only sand blown about by the wind. You see mountains of sand in one place, then you see they have moved to another." [11]

But Ibn Battuta's writings do contain a few geographic errors. Most notably, like Idrisi, he believed that the Niger was simply an arm of the Nile. Such errors were understandable. Ibn Battuta was less interested in the geographic features of the lands through which he passed than he was in the people who made the region their home. Accordingly, his account gives much more information on the foods, customs, and beliefs of the

West Africans than on the geography of the savanna and the Sahara. The main purpose of his trip was to describe the lives of the people he met, not to create an accurate map of his travels.

Passing the Baton

With the writings of Ibn Battuta, the early period of West African exploration came to a close. The Arabs, the Romans, the Greeks, and the Phoenicians all had investigated some parts of West Africa, and all had returned with valuable information about the region and its peoples. Among them, they had described the dry wastes of the Sahara and the more fertile soils of the savanna, the lives of the desert nomads and the glory that was Mali.

But much more remained. The course of the Niger was uncertain, the shape of the coastline wholly unknown. How far south the savanna extended was a mystery, and what lay below it, except in broadest outline, was a puzzle. Neither the great classical cultures nor the medieval Muslims had settled these questions. That challenge would be left, instead, to a new group of adventurers: the Portuguese mariners of the European Renaissance.

CHAPTER TWO

The West African Coast

Even by European standards, Portugal was not especially important during the medieval period. Tucked away in the extreme southwestern corner of the continent, Portugal was small, obscure, and generally ignored by other Europeans. While the country did export fish and a few other items, Portugal's capital city of Lisbon did not rank alongside the commercial centers of Italy or northern Germany. Nor could Lisbon match the cultural attainments of medieval cities such as Paris.

Yet despite its relative insignificance, Portugal was the first European nation to make a serious study of West African geography. Beginning in the early 1400s, Portuguese ships were a steady presence along the West African coastline. Slowly at first, and then with increasing enthusiasm, the mariners and adventurers of Portugal sailed down the shores of the unknown continent to the south, mapping, charting, and taking notes. The Portuguese would permanently change the way Europeans looked at the world beyond their borders, and they would permanently alter West African culture as well.

Prince Henry the Navigator

Portugal rose to prominence in exploration for several reasons. Perhaps the most obvious was the country's position at the edge of the Atlantic Ocean. Then as now, Portugal occupied a narrow strip of land along the sea. With relatively few other natural resources, the Portuguese turned to the sea for sustenance. Over time the Portuguese became hardy mariners. Few other Europeans could equal the Portuguese in the skills of sailing, shipbuilding, and navigation. These seafaring abilities made Portugal a likely candidate to lead the race into the unknown.

Moreover, Portugal's location encouraged its people to investigate West Africa. The southern coast of Portugal lies less than two hundred miles from Morocco; the Portuguese began their investigations by sailing along the nearby North African coast. From there, it made sense for inquisitive Portuguese explorers to follow the curve of the shore as it gradually dipped to the south and the equator. Certainly it was easier for the Portuguese to undertake this kind of expedition than it would have been for sailors from more distant countries, such as England or the Netherlands.

But the main reason Portugal took the lead among European countries had to do with the dreams of a member of the royal family. This was Prince Henry, often known as Henry the Navigator. Although trained as a warrior, Henry's true interests lay elsewhere. From an early age, he had been passionately interested in exploration and all that might lie outside the boundaries of the known world. Throughout his lifetime, he would devote much of his energy to investigating the mysteries of foreign lands.

A Quest for Gold

Prince Henry's interest in Africa probably began in 1415, when he was just twenty-one. From the early 700s, the Muslims of North Africa had held the upper hand in their dealings with Europeans. Both culturally and politically, they exercised a strong influence on life in Mediterranean Europe. Between 711 and the middle of the thirteenth century, for instance, Muslims had ruled all or parts of present-day Portugal and nearby Spain. Even after reclaiming this territory, Christian Europeans, in contrast, had no corresponding influence in north Africa.

During the fifteenth century, Prince Henry the Navigator of Portugal sponsored several dozen voyages of exploration along the West African coast.

In 1415, however, that lack of influence abruptly changed. That year, Henry and one of his brothers led an attack on the Muslim city of Ceuta in modern Morocco. They brought with them only five hundred soldiers, many of whom were killed in the fighting. Nevertheless, the battle continued, thanks in large part to the dedication of Henry himself. As one contemporary writer described it, Henry's "limbs were vigorous and his courage very great."[12] In the end, the Portuguese took Ceuta. For the first time since the fall of the Roman Empire, Europe controlled a piece of African territory.

Over the next few years, Henry served as governor of Ceuta. During this time, he did not extend Portuguese control much beyond the city, but he did become intrigued by the rest of the continent. Part of this interest was related to his long-standing desire for purely geographical knowledge. As the Portuguese chronicler Gomes Eannes de Azurara wrote in 1450, Henry's years in Ceuta awakened in him "a wish to know the land that lay beyond the isles of Canary,"[13] that is, the Canary Islands in the Atlantic Ocean off Africa's northwest coastline. Here, Henry thought, was an opportunity to find the answers to some of the great riddles of geography.

Henry's interest in Africa was also motivated by religion and politics. During his time and for many years earlier, hostility between Christians and Muslims had been more or less constant. As a devout Christian, Henry considered the Muslims' religious faith misguided and Islam itself his bitter enemy. Knowing that northern Africa, at least, was home to many Muslims, Henry was eager to determine the extent of Muslim power across the continent. As Azurara explained it, "Every wise man is obliged by natural prudence to wish for a knowledge of the power of his enemy."[14]

And Henry had economic concerns as well. He could not help but notice the variety of trade goods that came into Ceuta from points further to the south. In particular, he was intrigued by persistent and exciting rumors about a great country somewhere in the West African interior. This country, the Ceutans reported, had a never-ending supply of gold. The rumors were vague and uncertain, but the more Henry heard, the more eager he became. Somewhere in Africa was a place that held undreamed-of wealth, and Henry meant to find it.

The First Voyagers

The exact sequence of Portuguese exploration to the south is somewhat unclear. What is certain is that the process of exploration got off to a slow start. Despite his nickname, Henry was no sailor. He was content to organize expeditions from his court, which overlooked the Atlantic in extreme southwestern Portugal. As a result, Henry's understanding of foreign geography was dependent on the distance his sailors were willing to travel.

And at first, that was not far at all. Most of the men Henry sent out refused to venture more than a few dozen miles along the West African coast. To them, the Atlantic Ocean was dangerous and frightening, full of strange beasts and powerful currents. Nor were sailors comforted by the reports of Arab merchants and geographers who had visited the area by land. The Arabs, the sailors pointed out, called the Atlantic "the Green Sea of Darkness."[15] The sailors saw little likelihood of surviving a journey of the scope Henry longed for.

Still, Henry was not discouraged. When captains came back to tell him that they had lost their courage to continue, he simply outfitted another voyage and encouraged these sailors to continue a little further—even if only a few miles past the distance achieved by the previous crew. The strategy worked. Moving sometimes no more than ten or twelve miles beyond the previous voyagers, the explorers gradually pushed their way down the coast of present-day Morocco and Western Sahara. By 1430, the Portuguese sailors had made impressive progress.

But during the early 1430s, the pace of exploration began to slow. The problem was a place called Cape Bojador. Located in modern-day Western Sahara,

In this painting, Prince Henry (third from right, wearing hat) watches as a fleet of his ships returns from West Africa to Sagres in southwestern Portugal.

nearly a thousand miles southwest of Ceuta, the cape was barren and treacherous, and mariners assumed that conditions to its south were no better. "Beyond this Cape," wrote Azurara, summarizing the perspective of the seamen, "there is no race of men nor place of inhabitants. . . . There is no water, no tree, no green herb." The sea was too shallow for navigation, the currents too swift. "No ship having once passed the Cape," added Azurara, "will ever be able to return."[16]

The best seafarers of Portugal had made it this far, but now it seemed that they could go no further. In the opinion of the explorers, Cape Bojador was simply impassable. Harsh and inhospitable, it marked the end of the known world for these mariners. A succession of Portuguese explorers reached the cape, only to return home without attempting to round it. By the mid-1430s, as many as fourteen separate expeditions had turned back within sight of Cape Bojador. Henry's plans had stalled. It seemed that his search for wealth and knowledge might be at an end.

Beyond the Cape

Among the men who tried to round Cape Bojador was Gil Eanes, one of Henry's household servants and a skilled seaman in his own right. In 1433 Eanes made his first voyage in command of his own ship. He came as close to rounding Cape Bojador as any previous Portuguese captain, but at the last moment he was struck by a failure of nerve. As Eanes explained it to Henry after his return to Portugal, he could not quite dismiss the terrible tales he had heard from his fellow mariners about the menacing cape and what lay beyond it. Upon seeing the cape, he had abruptly decided that it would be foolish to go any further.

Henry was not dismayed. In 1434 he outfitted Eanes for another voyage. He chided his servant for his earlier readiness to believe the worst of the stories he had heard and assured Eanes that there must be some way around the cape. Henry also promised Eanes "honour and profit"[17] if he should manage to round the cape this time.

Whether because of the pep talk or the bribe, Eanes was successful. Conquering his own fears and those of his crew, Eanes sailed around Cape Bojador and continued some distance to the south. As earlier captains had predicted, the coast of this part of Africa was indeed wild and desolate. "Finding neither dwellings nor people," observed a commentator of the early 1500s, "nothing save sandy and arid land, [Eanes] turned back."[18] But although Eanes had seen no sign of human habitation, the land was not completely barren. At one point he ventured onto the coast, where he picked a few plant samples to take back to Portugal.

Eanes's triumphant return not only proved that the dangers of Cape Bojador had been indeed exaggerated but also indicated that further travel was feasible. In 1435 Eanes made a third voyage along the African coastline, this time accompanied by a captain named Afonso Baldaia.

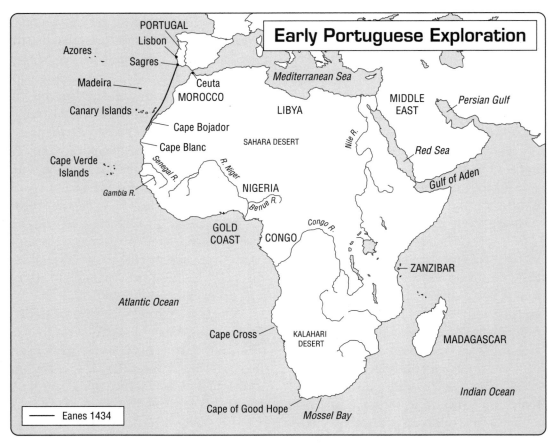

Early Portuguese Exploration

PORTUGAL
Lisbon
Azores
Sagres
Madeira
Ceuta
MOROCCO
Canary Islands
Cape Bojador
Cape Blanc
Cape Verde Islands
Senegal R.
Gambia R.
R. Niger
NIGERIA
Benue R.
GOLD COAST
CONGO
Congo R.
Mediterranean Sea
LIBYA
SAHARA DESERT
Nile R.
MIDDLE EAST
Persian Gulf
Red Sea
Gulf of Aden
ZANZIBAR
Atlantic Ocean
Cape Cross
KALAHARI DESERT
MADAGASCAR
Indian Ocean
Cape of Good Hope
Mossel Bay

——— Eanes 1434

The two men sailed about 150 miles south of Cape Bojador. They still saw no people, but on one visit to the mainland, Eanes and Baldaia spied the tracks of men and camels in the sand. Clearly the land was inhabited.

If Henry was pleased with the results of Eanes's 1434 journey around Cape Bojador, he was now thrilled to hear that people lived in this harsh and distant part of West Africa. "The inhabited region cannot be far off,"[19] Henry exulted upon hearing the news. In his mind the discovery of human footprints demonstrated the truth of the rumors he had

heard years earlier in Ceuta: that the great African desert was home to a fantastically wealthy people with an inexhaustible supply of gold. At last, Henry's drive and determination seemed to be bringing him close to his goal.

Knowledge and Profit

Henry lost no time in sending Eanes and Baldaia out again, this time with very specific orders. The men were to sail as far south as possible and make every effort to find signs of habitation. When they did, they were to approach the natives with an eye toward learning as much as they could about the local lands and peoples. Henry had little interest in establishing friendly ties with any Africans his commanders encountered. On the contrary, he urged Eanes and Baldaia to use violence and trickery. "Capture one of them, if possible," Henry's instructions continued. "To me it would be no small thing to have some man to tell me of this land."[20]

On this voyage the Portuguese sailors nearly reached Cape Blanc, about halfway along the West African bulge, before turning back. Along the way they successfully filled in another few hundred miles of shoreline on the growing European map of Africa. Moreover, when the ship anchored in a coastal bay, two members of the crew saddled a pair of horses brought for the purpose and rode a short distance into the interior. There they spotted a group of people among the sand dunes.

Eager to fulfill Henry's request for a native inhabitant who could describe the land and its peoples, they immediately tried to take the Africans prisoner. But when the two crewmen charged forward, the Africans fought back. The fighting, Azurara wrote, continued "until the sun began to give warning of night, on which account [the Europeans] went back to their ship."[21] They and their captains had to be content instead with bringing back the furs from a herd of sea lions, over five thousand of which they found at an inlet called Río de Oro, River of Gold, in present-day Western Sahara.

The sealskins became an important trading commodity for Portugal, but

Sea lions sun themselves on a beach. Skins from sea lions killed along the West African coast were an important trading commodity for Portugal during the fifteenth century.

Henry did not lose sight of his desire for gold—or for a native African who could guide his sailors to the source of the treasure. In 1441, an expedition led by Portuguese explorers Antao Goncalves and Nuno Tristao returned to the Río de Oro in search of more furs and human prisoners as well. Once again, the travelers scoured the dunes for potential captives. But this time, when they happened upon a small inland settlement, they took the inhabitants by surprise. Charging upon the Africans, they took ten prisoners, including a man they believed to be a local chief.

Goncalves and Tristao were delighted with their success. "Besides the knowledge that the Prince will gain," noted Tristao, "profit will accrue to him by their services or ransom."[22] Henry was indeed delighted to see the captives when they arrived in Portugal. Although they proved unwilling or unable to tell him much about Africa's gold, they did provide him with some useful information about the geography of their part of the continent. Better yet, from the Portuguese perspective, the captured Africans could be put to work. They became the first Africans to be enslaved by modern Europeans. They would not be the last.

The Slave Trade

The concept of slavery was an old one. Many, perhaps most, cultures throughout the world practiced it in some form. That list included many West African societies. Thus, there was already a thriving slave trade within the African interior. Ibn Battuta, among others, took part in this business. "When I came to Tadakka," Ibn Battuta wrote about a stop on his journey home from Mali, "I wanted to buy an educated slave woman."[23] After some haggling, he did exactly that.

A more important model for the Portuguese, however, was the example of the Hebrews of the biblical Old Testament. Most of the great Hebrew patriarchs had owned slaves. In fact, according to the Bible, slavery was not merely just, it was ordained as a positive good by God himself, as long as the enslaved were not Jews. As the book of Leviticus (25:44) put it, "Both thy bondmen, and thy bondmaids, which thou shalt have, shall be of the heathen that are round about you."

To the fifteenth-century Christians of Portugal, the Biblical precepts still held. Henry and his people had no difficulty justifying the enslavement of non-Christians. As far as the Portuguese were concerned, the people of Africa seemed supremely well qualified for slavery. The Old Testament told of Canaan, one of Noah's grandsons, whose descendants had been doomed to perpetual servitude. Christian traditions of the time held that Canaan's descendants had settled in Africa. Thus, the enslavement of Africans appeared doubly just. Doubts about the morality of their actions dogged Goncalves and Tristao not at all.

The realization that Africans could be bought and sold like so many sealskins helped spark a new interest in the continent among the Portuguese. Once,

The African View

The people of West Africa generally held a dim view of the Portuguese and those Europeans who followed them. There were good reasons for this dislike. As historian Timothy Severin writes in *The African Adventure:* "The white man, as the Negro saw him, was tarnished. West African merchants minted counterfeit spread eagle dollars for the native trade. Tricky surgeons sold ship's bilgewater [wastewater] as medicine." Lies, deceptions, and outright swindles were all too common among European traders.

This attitude prevailed for hundreds of years. Well into the 1700s, European merchants in the area consistently tried to get every cent they could out of the people of West Africa while giving up as little as possible in return. Former slave trader John Newton, best known today for writing the hymn "Amazing Grace," may have said it best. As he put it years later (quoted in Robin Hallett's *The Penetration of Africa*), "We have, I fear too deservedly, a very unfavourable character [reputation] along the coast."

In the short term, this deceitful behavior allowed the Europeans to make a quick fortune. In the longer run, however, the traders' actions were not only immoral; they were foolish. The more the Europeans swindled and lied, the more the West Africans resented their presence—and the more hostility later explorers encountered.

Henry had found it hard to encourage captains and crewmen to venture south along the African coastline. But as soon as the value of the slave trade became evident, traffic down Africa's western shoreline began to boom. Hoping to make their fortunes, merchants and explorers alike hurried to make their own voyages south.

At first, Portuguese adventurers traveled haphazardly around the capes and bays of West Africa, looking for potential captives. By 1448, however, Henry had established a combined fortress and trading post on the island of Arguin, off Cape Blanc. Staffed by Portuguese traders and officials, it served as a center for the increasingly organized trade in African slaves. No longer did armed groups of Europeans capture slaves on their own, as Goncalves and Tristao had done. Now the Portuguese found it much more efficient to barter for slaves, either with Arab traders in the area or with West African peoples who had taken slaves for themselves.

Cadamosto

With the coming of the slave trade, the pace of exploration increased. New adventurers investigated bays, river mouths,

West Africans captured for the slave trade are bound and yoked together as they march to slave ships.

and islands noted but not studied by the first Portuguese to come through the area. Others pushed farther south, searching for new sources of slaves along with other goods such as spices, ivory, and gold. In 1445, Dinís Dias sailed to the mouth of the Senegal River; a year later, Tristao reached the mouth of the Gambia River, more than a hundred miles farther south. By 1448 Portuguese navigators had rounded the bulge of Africa. Only fifteen years earlier, Cape Bojador had seemed an insurmountable barrier. Now there seemed to be no limit to the distance the Portuguese could travel.

Among the greatest of this new generation of explorers was a man named Alvise da Cadamosto. Originally from Venice, Cadamosto had become friendly with Henry and had earned the Portuguese prince's backing for two journeys of exploration, probably in 1454 and 1456. To Cadamosto, however, purely geographic knowledge was not important. He had other purposes instead. "My constant attention," he wrote, "was in the first place to acquire wealth, and secondly to procure fame." [24] As a former merchant himself, Cadamosto had every expectation that West Africa would be the place for him to reach these goals.

Nevertheless, Cadamosto was eager for adventure and hopeful of making new discoveries. At one point, for instance, he insisted on traveling up the Gambia River. A few miles past the river's mouth, however, a group of Africans attacked the explorer and his men. The Europeans fired back with powerful crossbows, wounding and killing several of their attackers. Cadamosto was all for continuing the journey, preferably for a hundred miles or more, "in the hope of finding better disposed peoples."[25] But when his men refused to continue, Cadamosto reluctantly turned back. Even so, he was probably the first European to lead a voyage into the river.

Cadamosto's fame lay less in his discoveries, though, than in the accounts he published of his voyages. He was a keen observer and a careful writer with a strong interest in describing the natural features of the continent. Cape Blanc, he wrote, was "sandy and white, without

The Slave Trade

Slaves were among the first commodities to be shipped along the trade routes that sprang up across the Sahara between West Africa and the Middle East. For years the slave trade was vital. By some estimates, over 9 million men, women, and children were taken across the desert between 800 and 1800. Despite many deaths along the way, the trade proved extremely profitable. The people of North Africa and the Middle East proved just as eager to buy West Africans as they were to buy gold and spices.

In one sense, the arrival of the Europeans did not change the slave trade all that much. While estimates vary, the number of slaves purchased by Europeans for the Americas was similar to the number sent to northern Africa and the Middle East. And while the journey across the Atlantic was miserable—slaves were typically packed in tight, disease-ridden quarters at the bottom of a ship—it is not clear that the death rate was any higher than for those who crossed the Sahara.

The Europeans did have an enormous impact on the slave trade, however. For one, the 9 million or so slaves who went to the New World were captured and shipped across the Atlantic in the space of just a few hundred years. And, slaves who went north had a better chance of eventually earning freedom than did those in the New World. The conditions of slavery seem to have generally been better for slaves who wound up in Egypt or Morocco than for those who were taken to Haiti or Brazil. The workload, in particular, was brutal on a typical New World sugar plantation. Many slaves who survived the voyage to the Americas succumbed to exhaustion, overwork, and mistreatment.

signs of grass and trees whatsoever."[26] Similarly, Cadamosto was quite impressed by the Jeba River, also known as the Rio Grande. It was "at least twenty miles and upwards in breadth," he observed, and "very beautiful green trees were to be seen on the other part of the land to the south."[27]

But Cadamosto was also intrigued by the people he met and observed. He was fascinated by the economy of the area and the complexity of the trade routes that led through the interior. Although he did not penetrate too far into the interior, he nevertheless learned a great deal about the trade in salt, gold, and other commodities brought to the coasts from inland areas. He also wrote detailed observations of the way West Africans lived. He described the women of the Wolof people, for example, as "much inclined to singing and dancing," but added that "they never dance except by moonlight."[28]

Cadamosto described the weapons, the food, the marriage customs, and much more of the people he visited. Like Ibn Battuta, some of what he saw he found admirable; other things he viewed with distaste. Occasionally he had both reactions at the same time. "The men and women are clean in their persons, since they wash themselves all over four or five times a day," he wrote of one culture, "but in eating they are filthy and ill-mannered."[29] Whether his impressions were positive or negative, however, Cadamosto always maintained a lively curiosity about the people he saw. No other explorer of his time could match the picture he gave of coastal West Africa in the middle of the fifteenth century.

The Rest of the Coast

In the decades after Cadamosto's voyages, Portuguese ships ranged ever farther along the West African coastline. About 1457, Diogo Gomes traveled some distance up the Gambia River—as much as a few hundred miles by some accounts. Even the death of Prince Henry in 1460 did not reduce interest in exploration. In 1462, Pero de Sintra became the first Portuguese navigator to sail along the coast of Sierra Leone. (The name of the region, which means "lion mountains," stemmed from de Sintra's observation that thunderclaps in the coastal mountains sounded like the roars of lions.) By this time, about two thousand miles of the West African coast had been explored.

Even that was not enough for the Portuguese commanders. On they traveled, past present-day Liberia and the Ivory Coast. The coastline gradually ceased running north–south and instead led the explorers almost due east. Successive expeditions journeyed in waves along the coastlines of Ghana, Benin, and Nigeria, each traveling past the limits of the one before. In 1473 Fernando Po reached the Bight of Biafra on the border between Nigeria and Cameroon, where the shore begins to veer once again toward the south. Nine years later, Diogo Cão traveled past Cameroon to the Congo River in

The Elephant and the Hippopotamus

Portuguese travelers were deeply intrigued by the wildlife of West Africa. Cadamosto, for example, was intrigued by the elephant and the hippopotamus (the latter of which he called "river horse," the translation of hippopotamus *from Greek). This description appears in his book,* The Voyages of Cadamosto.

I wish it to be understood that the foot of the elephant is round, almost like the foot of the horse, but the foot has not a hoof like the horse, but is all a black, thick, callosity [calloused skin]; around this there are five claws, level with the ground. . . . Do not believe that the elephant cannot bend its knees, as I have heard said at times; on the contrary, the animal moves, bends, and rises like any other animal. . . . [The hippopotamus] lives now on the land, now in the water, and maintains itself in both elements. It is formed thus—its body, the size of a cow's, with short limbs, has cleft feet, and its head is shaped like a horse's, with two large tusks, as a wild boar has. . . . The like has not been found in any other parts to which we Christians have sailed, save these countries of the Blacks.

The Portuguese explorer Cadamosto was fascinated with the elephants (pictured) and hippopotamuses he observed during his voyages.

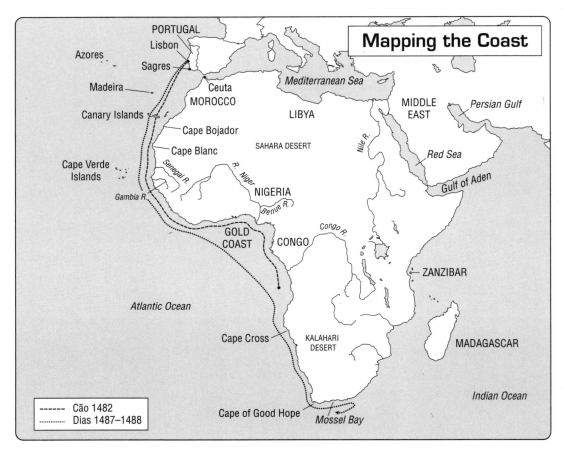

Mapping the Coast

PORTUGAL
Lisbon
Azores
Sagres
Madeira
Ceuta
MOROCCO
Canary Islands
Cape Bojador
Cape Blanc
Cape Verde
Islands
Senegal R.
Gambia R.
Mediterranean Sea
LIBYA
SAHARA DESERT
Nile R.
R. Niger
NIGERIA
Benue R.
GOLD
COAST
CONGO
Congo R.
MIDDLE
EAST
Persian Gulf
Red Sea
Gulf of Aden
ZANZIBAR
Atlantic Ocean
Cape Cross
KALAHARI
DESERT
MADAGASCAR
Indian Ocean
Cape of Good Hope
Mossel Bay

------ Cão 1482
.... Dias 1487–1488

south central Africa, and Bartholomeu Dias reached the Cape of Good Hope, at the southern tip of Africa, shortly afterward. The Portuguese had explored the entire West African coastline.

To be sure, there was a great deal about West Africa that the Portuguese did not yet know. Portuguese sailors had sped past many important landforms and natural features without doing more than noting their presence. They had made few inroads into the interior, and had spent little time ashore. They produced no great maps of the region and, other than Cadamosto and a few others, wrote no detailed accounts of their experiences. Yet the Portuguese adventurers had nevertheless completed a remarkable achievement. They had sailed thousands of miles into the unknown, and they had added immeasurably to European knowledge of the outside world.

CHAPTER THREE

The Search for the River Niger

Diogo Cão's voyage past Cameroon did not mark the end of West African exploration by any means. For years to come, the Portuguese would continue to be a powerful commercial presence along the coast. Spices, ivory, and gold remained powerful attractions; so too did the slave trade, especially as Portugal expanded its influence into Latin America. By the early 1500s ships loaded with African captives were regularly making their way across the Atlantic from West Africa to the sugar plantations of the New World.

By this time, though, Portugal was no longer the only European power with an interest in West Africa. Hopeful of sharing in West Africa's riches, mariners from other European nations descended on the region. France, England, and the Netherlands, in particular, were eager to win parts of the West African trade. Though the Portuguese had a head start, they could not keep away the interlopers. Before long, ship captains from these three nations were making regular voyages to West Africa and returning with goods of their own.

The Europeans who went to West Africa during the 1500s and 1600s were primarily merchants, and they were generally content to stay in the known parts of the region. Occasionally, traders in search of new markets would venture up a coastal river or sail into an unfamiliar bay. A few of these adventurers reported their discoveries in some detail. Richard Jobson of England, who journeyed over four hundred miles up the Gambia River in 1621, was particularly interested in the river's enormous crocodiles. "The people of the Country stand in such dread of these," Jobson reported, "that they dare not wash their hands in the great River, much lesse offer to swimme or wade therein."[30]

But Jobson was unusual. For the most part, the representatives of the great European powers stayed along the coasts instead of undertaking exploration into the interior. As a result, European understanding of West African geography changed scarcely at all during this time. "The Portuguese struck six hundred miles into Ethiopia [in East Africa] a few weeks after arriving there," says historian Timothy Severin, "but the Europeans in West Africa three centuries later were still, effectively, on the beach."[31] Not until the late 1700s would the European powers launch a serious journey into the West African interior.

"A Hideous People"

The process of exploration stalled for several reasons, but a lack of curiosity was not among them. European geographers of the period were deeply interested in learning more about the West African interior. Traders, too, were eager

Captured Africans sit packed together on the deck of a slave ship. Such ships were used to transport slaves for sale in European and New World markets.

to discover the sources of African goods for themselves. "[Africa] gives us gold, ivory, wax, hides, sugar, pepper," wrote one Portuguese observer of the time, "and it would give us more things if we would only penetrate into the hinterland." [32]

The perceived dangers of the West African interior kept people from traveling beyond the coast, however. The unfamiliar climate, vegetation, and animal life intimidated many of the merchants, who preferred to stay on the coast and have their trading partners come to them. The ocean, at least, was recognizable even so far south, and staying with the ships made a quick getaway possible.

Moreover, Europeans were leery of the West Africans themselves. If the countryside was foreign to the Europeans who visited the region, the people of the area were more foreign still. The Christian Europeans of the time considered themselves the most civilized people on earth, and many of them reacted to the ways of other cultures with disapproval and disgust. Polygamy, nudity, body ornamentation—all common in parts of West Africa—outraged travelers or fueled their claims of superiority. "They are a hideous people," summed up one English writer about a group that lived along the Ivory Coast, "and stink exceedingly." [33]

Not all traders held these views. Dutch trader William Bosman was more complimentary than many when he wrote about his impressions of people living in a place called Fida. "They are so civil to each other," Bosman wrote in comments that were published in 1704, "and the Inferiour so respectful to the Superiour, that at first I was very much surprised at it." The work ethic of these people, Bosman added, was admirable as well. As he put it, "Men as well as Women are . . . vigorously Industrious and Laborious." [34]

But most Europeans in the region saw the Africans as little more than savages. During the years of coastal trading, frequent battles broke out between Europeans and Africans. Thanks to their superior weapons, the Europeans often emerged victorious. "The negros would have beaten the company [crew] from the shore," reported English captain William Towerson in 1557, referring to his crew's attempt to land, "whereupon the company resisted them, and slew and hurt divers [many] of them, and, having put them to flight, burned their towne and brake [broke] all their boats." [35]

Not all battles, however, ended with a European victory. At these times, Europeans tended to see themselves as victims. In their view, the Africans staged attacks without reason or justification, a perspective that ignored the reality of the slave trade and skipped over the fact that Europeans were taking islands and tramping over lands previously claimed by local peoples. The fear of attack, in any case, was constant for many European travelers; Europeans typically looked on the West Africans with suspicion and distrust.

West Africans like this man decorated their bodies with paint, a practice Europeans regarded with contempt.

"Smothering Heate"

More significant, however, were the problems of climate and disease. Much of West Africa was brutally hot, and the tropical forest was humid as well. Few Europeans were prepared for the intense climate. "Smothering heate with close and cloudie aire," complained an early English traveler to Benin. "Weather of

such putrefying quality that it rotted the coates off [the travelers'] backs."[36] The heat sapped travelers' energy, and in the days before air conditioning and electric fans, there was no escape.

Worse, insofar as Europeans were concerned, West Africa was a hotbed for malaria, yellow fever, and other tropical diseases. Some Africans had a natural immunity to some of these illnesses, but Europeans largely did not. As a result, most European travelers who stayed any length of time in West Africa became sick. The diseases were serious indeed, with terrible fevers that could last for weeks. Often they brought death. "Many of our men fell sicke," wrote William Towerson at one point in his trip to Guinea. "Sixe of them died."[37]

Today it is known that malaria and yellow fever are carried by mosquitoes, but during the early years of European exploration, travelers looked elsewhere for a cause. Some blamed the heat and the wet, humid air of West Africa, particularly in the forests and swamps just off the coast. If heat and humidity were at fault, it made sense for European arrivals to stay on their ships or on offshore islands, where winds blew and the damaging effects of the climate would be limited. In contrast, to venture into the interior, where forests and swamps were everywhere, was to commit suicide.

Perhaps more than any other reason, the fear of disease kept the Portuguese from traveling inland. According to sixteenth-century Portuguese traveler

João de Barros, the possibility of illness was the only reason. In Barros's eyes, the scourge of disease had been ordained by God. To keep Europeans out of the African interior, he wrote, God "had placed a striking angel with a flaming sword of deadly fevers" [38] to block European passage into West Africa's hinterlands. Whether its origin was natural or divinely inspired, the "sword of deadly fevers" was extraordinarily successful. Until the late 1700s, it kept nearly all Europeans from exploring the interior.

The African Association

The desire to know more about West Africa thus lay dormant for many years. But in the late 1700s, after years of inaction, interest in reaching the interior suddenly awakened. The spark was a revolution in European thought, known today as the Enlightenment. Europeans of the Enlightenment were eager for scientific knowledge. For years, they believed, Europe had been prone to superstitious thinking; it had seen the world as an arbitrary and illogical place. Now the emphasis was on reason: the

Mosquitoes in West Africa transmitted deadly tropical diseases like malaria and yellow fever to Europeans, who had no natural immunity to these illnesses.

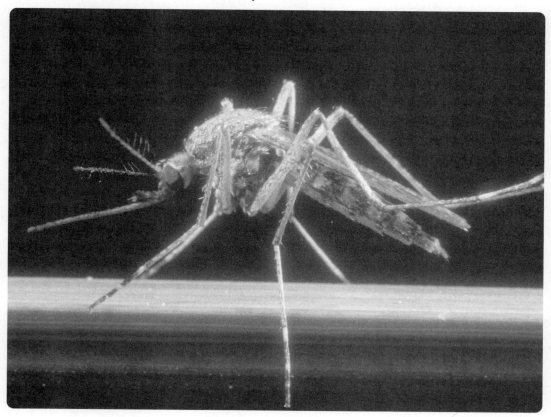

ability of humankind to think clearly, objectively, and scientifically.

Early in the Enlightenment, explorers from countries such as England and France had ventured into previously unknown areas of the globe. English sea captain James Cook had traveled to Australia, Antarctica, and the islands of the South Pacific, not so much for economic gain as to satisfy a curiosity about the location of oceans and continents. Others had followed. Their purpose was to make accurate maps, describe the land and seas

Naturalist Joseph Banks served as chairman of England's African Association beginning in 1788.

they encountered, and undertake scientific studies of the peoples, animals, and plants.

It was not long before Enlightenment thinkers turned their attention to West Africa. In 1788, ten years after Cook embarked on his third and final Pacific voyage, a group of English gentlemen established a club for the purpose of African exploration. Called the Association for Promoting the Discovery of the Interior Districts of Africa, it was better known simply as the African Association. It was chaired by Joseph Banks, a naturalist and explorer who had been a member of Cook's first expedition, and it included several other men whose names would have been well known to the English upper and middle classes of the time.

The members of the African Association had many interests. Above all they wanted to know about the River Niger. Europeans knew only that this river was large and flowed somewhere through west-central Africa. Vague scraps of knowledge had come to Europe from Muslim travelers—including, perhaps, Ibn Battuta, who had visited it in 1352—and from the writings of Herodotus. But important questions remained. Where did the Niger begin, and where did it end? Did it flow east, as Herodotus had maintained, or west? Perhaps it was an arm of the Nile, as Idrisi had believed; or perhaps it connected to the Senegal River, as some Portuguese explorers suspected. The men of the African Association itched to find out.

Simon Lucas

Immediately after its formation in June 1788, the African Association agreed to sponsor two separate expeditions to locate the River Niger. One of these expeditions was Ledyard's. The other was to be led by a man named Simon Lucas. Lucas had an interesting background. Early in his life he had been captured by pirates off the North African seacoast and sold into slavery in Morocco. Three years later, fluent in Arabic and well versed in African ways, Lucas was ransomed by his government and given a job as an interpreter.

This background made Lucas one of the best qualified Englishmen to undertake a West African journey. With this in mind, the association assigned him to go to Tripoli in modern Libya and make his way south into the desert. Unfortunately, Lucas had little real interest in exploration or geography. Though he spent nearly a year in Tripoli, he never traveled more than a few miles south of the city.

First Attempts

Getting started, however, proved more difficult than Banks and his fellow association members anticipated. Their first choice as the leader of an expedition to the Niger was John Ledyard, an American who had also been a member of one of Cook's expeditions. Ledyard intended to begin in Cairo, Egypt. From there he would follow Arab trade routes across the Sahara to the Niger. Ledyard traveled to Cairo as scheduled and began making preparations for the trip. But before the trip got under way, he caught dysentery and died.

The association quickly appointed a new expedition leader, British army officer Daniel Houghton, and assigned him to follow a different route, one that would begin at the mouth of the Gambia River and head east. He was given a list of fifty-four questions to answer about the river and its surroundings. Some were purely geographical: "In what country does [the Niger] rise?" "Through what countries does it pass?" Other questions were concerned with the economic, religious, and political accomplishments of the people of the region: "Are written receipts given when Lands are sold?"[39]

In 1790 Houghton headed off into the wilderness, taking with him the list of questions and an assortment of trade goods—enough to require a horse, five donkeys, and a servant to help him with the load. At first Houghton's journey was relatively straightforward: Although he met with some initial hostility, he journeyed deeper into the interior and seemed to be making good progress. One friendly ruler at Medina, about a hundred miles up the Gambia River, assured Houghton that he would have no difficulty reaching the Niger.

But as time went on, conditions became much more problematic. The weather was wet and the paths hard to follow. An accidental fire destroyed many of his trade goods; the king of a country called Bondou robbed him of most of what remained. Even his interpreter deserted him. Nevertheless, Houghton struggled on until he reached about six hundred miles inland, further than any previous European explorer is known to have ventured. There, alone and defenseless, he was robbed and killed by a group of Muslim traders. Native Africans quickly spread word of Houghton's fate throughout the region. Before long, details of his death had reached Europeans on the coast.

Despite the tragic end to Houghton's life, his journey had not been in vain. At intervals along his route, he had written letters to his superiors in the African Association, and these letters revealed important information about the West African interior. Although he had not reached the Niger, he had learned in his discussions with local peoples that it was not the same river as the Senegal. Moreover, his information strongly suggested that the Niger flowed east, just as Herodotus had believed. Still, no European had set eyes on the mighty river. It was time for the African Association to try once more.

Mungo Park

The organization's choice this time was a young Scotsman with the unusual name of Mungo Park. Born in 1771, Park had been trained as a doctor, but his true

Scotsman Mungo Park volunteered to lead an expedition into the African interior in 1795.

interests lay in exploration and in the natural world. In 1792 he had gotten to know Joseph Banks, the head of the African Association. By all accounts, the young explorer made a good impression on Banks. Two years later, when Park volunteered to lead a new African expedition, the committee accepted his application. In May 1795, Park left England and sailed for the Gambia River.

Park's mission was essentially the same as Houghton's. Like Houghton, he

Presents and Bribes

The story of the exploration of interior West Africa is in large part the story of presents and bribes. During the early nineteenth century, no single large power held control over wide stretches of West Africa. Instead, a succession of small kingdoms and principalities held sway. As travelers such as Mungo Park made their way across the region, they were constantly crossing borders into new territories. To smooth their way, many of them found it necessary to offer presents to the rulers of these unfamiliar lands. The giving of presents was common in West African societies; it indicated that the giver was friendly and respectful.

Generally, the explorers who participated in this tradition did not mind giving gifts. However, at times they resented the custom. Any presents larger than beads added considerably to the weight of the baggage and made the travelers' belongings more attractive to robbers. In addition, the exchange often felt less like a free-will offering than like a bribe, paid to a ruler to avoid imprisonment or to guarantee safe conduct through the ruler's territory. And some rulers were quite insistent on being rewarded in ways that they saw fit, often by requesting more items than those the explorers offered. "The request of an African prince," mused Mungo Park at one point in his *Travels in the Interior Districts of Africa,* "comes little short of a command. It is only a way of obtaining by gentle means, what he can, if he pleases, take by force."

European explorers often used beads to bribe West African rulers to guarantee safe passage through unfamiliar territories.

was to start at the Gambia River and continue east until he reached the Niger. There was one important difference, however. Suspecting that Houghton might have been killed for the trading goods he carried, the association took steps to make sure that Park traveled light. Whereas Houghton had taken plenty linens, beads, cloth, knives, and other materials, Park limited himself mainly to the supplies he would need and just enough trading goods to buy more food as he continued on his way.

Park was aware of the dangers of the trek, but he had the utmost confidence in himself and his abilities. "I knew that I was able to bear fatigue," he wrote in his account of his journey, "and I relied on my youth, and the strength of my constitution, to preserve me from the effects of the climate."[40] But Park was also cautious. Arriving in Gambia in July 1795, he spent five months along the seacoast, adjusting to the climate and waiting for the end of the rainy season.

During these months, Park did not sit still. He spent his time learning Mandingo, a language common in that part of West Africa. He also interviewed many traders to find out about what might lie inland. He was disappointed in their answers; he found them to be evasive and contradictory. "These circumstances," he wrote later on, "increased my anxiety to ascertain the truth from my own personal observation."[41] In December, when the rainy season ended, Park was at last ready to find out for himself.

The Journey Begins

Like Houghton, Park enjoyed his early travels, which took him through countries dominated by black Africans rather than the lighter-skinned Arabic speakers who lived further north. Although Park held many of the same racial prejudices as his European contemporaries, he genuinely liked most of these people and acknowledged the traits they shared with members of his own culture. "Whatever difference there is between the Negro and European in the conformation of the nose and the colour of the skin," he wrote, "there is none in the genuine sympathies and characteristic feelings of our common nature."[42]

The trip was by no means easy. In one kingdom, a party of horsemen tried to steal one of Park's guns when he stopped for the night. Later, the riders surrounded him and demanded payment before allowing him to move on. Regaining his freedom cost Park about half his possessions. A few days later, the ruler of another land took half of the remainder. The king of Bondou, who had taken most of Houghton's goods some time earlier, also did not let Park off easily. When Park offered him an umbrella as a present, the king insisted on taking his coat as well.

His load much lighter than before, Park now continued eastward to the country of Kaarta, close to five hundred miles inland. There a friendly king gave him some advice. War was imminent in the region, he explained; Park should give up his dream and turn back. But when the single-minded Park refused, the king offered an alternative. The war, he mused, might not involve countries to the north. Instead of continuing east, Park might head north and take a round-about route to the Niger. This path presented dangers of its own, he explained, but it seemed Park's only chance of success.

Park decided to try. In February 1796 he arrived in Ludamar, near the present-day border between Mali and Mauritania. Ludamar was dominated by Muslim traders who seemed to resent Park's presence among them. As he moved across the country, traders spit at him, mocked him, and took what few possessions he had left. "From the staring wildness of their eyes," Park wrote, "a stranger would immediately set them down as a nation of lunatics."[43]

Matters soon came to a head. On March 7, a group of Muslim horsemen arrived at Park's encampment and took him prisoner. They forced him to ride to a place called Benowm, where they tied him up and showered him with insults and abuse. His captors often deprived him of food; sometimes they forced him to drink from the cattle trough. Park considered an escape attempt, but for weeks no possibility presented itself. He was far too closely guarded, and the local king, who had ordered his capture, had threatened to have Park shot on sight if he tried.

Within a few months, the attention of his captors was diverted to other concerns, most notably a war with their neighbors.

Park was moved from Benowm to another site, and then to a third, this one a town called Jarra. Early in July, while he and his guards were being evacuated from Jarra in advance of enemy troops, he saw an opportunity to escape. Sneaking out of his tent at midnight, Park climbed onto his horse—almost the only thing he had been allowed to keep—and rode off into the desert.

Mungo Park's captors treat the explorer with contempt by forcing him to shave the head of an Arab boy.

To the Niger

Once there he found himself in a desperate situation. "I had not one single bead," he noted, "nor any other article of value in my possession, to purchase victuals [food] for myself, or corn for my horse."[44] Nevertheless, he determined to keep heading south and slightly east, toward the Niger, rather than to make his way immediately to the more familiar lands to the west. The great river was his goal, and he meant to find it no matter what the cost.

For the next week Park suffered mightily as he made his way through the desert. Tired and weary, he traveled largely at night. Mosquitoes plagued him; the howls of wild animals kept him in a state of nervous excitement. Although worried about hostility from the region's Muslim inhabitants, he was forced to approach the homes of shepherds and farmers along the way to beg for food and water. Park was surprised by the willingness of the people to share their meager resources.

After escaping his captors, Park stops to consider his desperate situation as he makes his way across the desert toward the Niger.

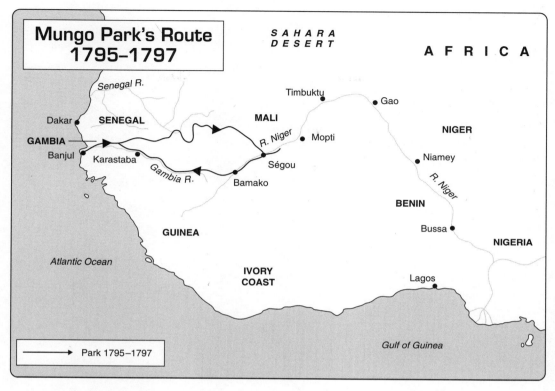

Mungo Park's Route 1795–1797

SAHARA DESERT

AFRICA

Senegal R.

Timbuktu • Gao

Dakar • SENEGAL MALI NIGER

GAMBIA R. Niger • Mopti

Banjul Karastaba Séamab Niamey

Gambia R. Bamako R. Niger

BENIN

GUINEA Bussa •

NIGERIA

Atlantic Ocean

IVORY COAST Lagos •

Gulf of Guinea

→ Park 1795–1797

His circumstances eventually improved. By accident, Park met with a group of travelers who offered to include him in their caravan. Park seized on the invitation; the travelers would provide a measure of protection and could serve as guides. Gradually, the group moved further and further south. His horse could no longer carry his weight, so Park was forced to walk. Still he pushed on, for he knew the river was near.

At last, on the morning of July 20, one of Park's fellow travelers caught his attention as they crossed a marsh. "Looking forwards," wrote Park,

I saw with infinite pleasure the great object of my mission: the long sought for, majestic Niger, glittering to the morning sun, as broad as the Thames [the river that flows through London] at Westminster, and flowing slowly to the *eastward*. I hastened to the brink, and, having drank of the water, lifted up my fervent thanks in prayer, to the Great Ruler of all things, for having thus far crowned my endeavours with success.[45]

Return to Gambia

Park was impressed by the size and beauty of the river and its surroundings. He soon entered the riverbank city of Ségou, which he estimated had a population

An African man and his sons fish a river in Ségou in Mali. Park was deeply impressed with the magnificence of eighteenth-century Ségou.

of about thirty thousand. The people were curious and friendly; one local ruler gave him some money when he discovered Park's impoverished situation. "The view of this extensive city," wrote Park, "the numerous canoes upon the river; the crowded population, and the cultivated state of the surrounding country, formed altogether a prospect of civilization and magnificence, which I little expected to find in the bosom of Africa."[46]

Park had hoped to continue his journey by following the Niger as far downstream as possible. But his weakened condition, combined with rainy weather, lack of trade goods, and fear of Muslims downstream, persuaded him to return to Gambia after venturing only a few dozen miles further along the great river. This time, Park decided to head straight west, avoiding the desert country where he had been held captive. The journey included yet another robbery and a bout of malaria that held Park up for seven months. He arrived in Gambia in June 1797 and finally reached London on Christmas Day.

The African Association was startled to see Park. Most of its members had

"A Negro Song"

Mungo Park's journey through the West African countryside struck a chord among the people of England. Indeed, Park's breathless tales of drama and danger inspired his fellow English citizens to compose poetic accounts of his adventures. Among these was this poem, called "A Negro Song," quoted in Park's Travels in the Interior Districts of Africa. *The poem was written by Georgiana, the Duchess of Devonshire, and it was a response to the help Park received in the days between his escape from captivity and his arrival at the River Niger.*

The loud wind roar'd, the rain fell fast;
The White Man yielded to the blast:
He sat him down, beneath our tree;
For weary, sad, and faint was he;
And ah, no wife, or mother's care,
For him, the milk or corn prepare:
    The White Man, shall our pity share;
    Alas, no wife or mother's care,
    For him, the milk or corn prepare.
The storm is o'er; the tempest past;
And Mercy's voice has hushed the blast.
The wind is heard in whispers low;
The White Man, far away must go;—
But ever in his heart will bear
Remembrance of the Negro's care.
    Go, White Man, go;—but with thee bear
    The Negro's wish, the Negro's prayer;
    Remembrance of the Negro's care.

given the explorer up for lost. They were delighted to be proved wrong, especially when Park began describing his experiences. He had survived fever, capture, robbery, and abuse—and he had returned with valuable information about vast stretches of West Africa. He had seen the Niger and determined its direction; he had made observations of the lands and peoples that surrounded it. Through his wits, courage, and determination, Park had become the first European to visit the great West African interior—and to return to tell the tale.

CHAPTER FOUR

The Mouth of the Niger

Park's achievement fired the imaginations of Europeans, especially the English. His adventures were impressive, and his discoveries great indeed. Still, questions remained. Europeans wondered whether it was feasible to reach the Niger from the north, as John Ledyard had originally planned before his death in Egypt. They wanted to know more about the people of the region and the civilization along the river's shores that Park had described. And they were eager to know where the mighty Niger reached its end.

This last question was of particular interest to scientifically minded Europeans. Geographers and other scholars debated the question endlessly. Now that the Niger's eastward flow had been established, many believed that the river continued across central Africa to join the Nile. Others argued instead that the river twisted south and east to meet the Congo River which flowed into the Atlantic about five hundred miles south of Cameroon. Still others believed that the Niger emptied into a series of swamps somewhere in the interior or evaporated in the hot sun of the Sahara.

There was one other possibility, but few people took it seriously. German geographer C.G. Reichard, one of the few, contended that the Niger continued east for a few hundred miles past Ségou, the city Park had visited, and then plunged south to exit into the Atlantic somewhere in present-day Nigeria. Reichard's contention, however, was scorned by most of his colleagues, in part because that part of the coast had no great rivers, only estuaries, swamps, and streams. "The hypothesis of Mr. Reichard," summed up influential English politician John Barrow, "is entitled to very little attention."[47]

Exploration and Tragedy

But geographers and explorers alike were determined to find out more about the Niger, and in the years after Park's journey several other expeditions set out to do just that. The first of these was undertaken by a German explorer named Friedrich Hornemann. Even while Park was still struggling toward the Niger, the African Association had assigned Hornemann to travel to the river following the desert route that Ledyard had planned to take.

Knowing of Park's difficulties with Muslim traders, Hornemann decided to disguise himself as a Muslim merchant while on his trek. He studied Arabic until he spoke it with near fluency, and he devoted months to learning the customs of the Arab merchants who made up the Sahara trading caravans. He adopted Muslim religious rituals and ate the Arabs' unfamiliar food as well. "At first," he wrote, "I did not relish the dried locusts, but [once] accustomed, grew fond of them." Their flavor he likened to "red herrings, but more delicious."[48]

In July 1798 Hornemann set out across the desert, traveling first to Murzuq in present-day Libya and then turning south toward the Niger. According to accounts of Africans who met him along the way, Hornemann reached Lake Chad with a caravan, then traveled west to the town of Bokani, only a day's journey from the Niger. But in Bokani, before he could reach the river, Hornemann caught a fever and died. His notes were lost, and with it the details of his discoveries.

A few years later Mungo Park returned to West Africa in an attempt to seek the mouth of the Niger. This expedition was very different from the first he had undertaken. This time, Park took with him forty-four Europeans, including thirty

A herd of cattle in Mali drinks from the Benue River, the main tributary of the River Niger. Eighteenth-century Europeans were determined to locate the mouth of the Niger.

soldiers in full dress uniform. Beginning once more at the mouth of the Gambia, Park and his entourage set out eastward. In August 1805, after struggling through the forests of West Africa, Park at last reached the Niger at the town of Bamako, about a hundred miles west of Ségou.

By this time, however, most of Park's companions were dead, the victims of malaria and dysentery. The few who survived journeyed downstream past Ségou to the town of Sansanding in modern-day Mali. There, half the remaining Europeans succumbed to disease. Neverthe-less, Park did not give up. In November 1805, he and his four remaining men built a forty-foot canoe and sailed downriver in hopes of reaching the Niger's mouth. They never returned.

Park's fate was a mystery for many years, but as had been the case with Hornemann, it eventually proved possible to reconstruct his final journey. The group had traveled a remarkable eight hundred miles down the Niger. But when the travelers reached Bussa in present-day Nigeria, they were attacked by a hostile army. The men tumbled out of their boat

In 1798 German explorer Friedrich Hornemann disguised himself as an Arab merchant and set out across the Sahara with a camel caravan like this one.

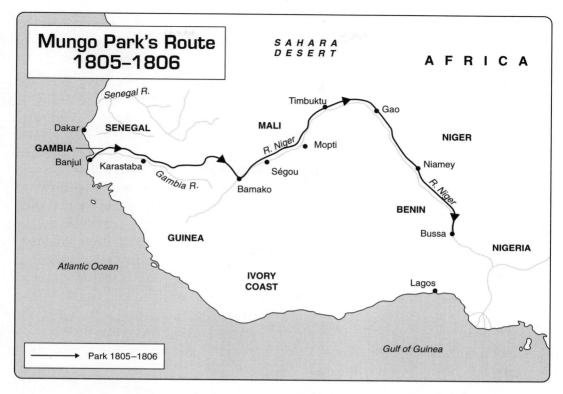

Mungo Park's Route 1805–1806

SAHARA DESERT

AFRICA

Senegal R.

Timbuktu

Gao

Dakar

SENEGAL

MALI

R. Niger

Mopti

NIGER

GAMBIA

Banjul

Karastaba

Gambia R.

Ségou

Niamey

Bamako

R. Niger

GUINEA

BENIN

Bussa

NIGERIA

Atlantic Ocean

IVORY COAST

Lagos

Gulf of Guinea

→ Park 1805–1806

and were drowned. Park's records, like those of Hornemann, were lost forever.

A third expedition, this one led by Englishmen George Lyon and James Ritchie, was scarcely more successful. In 1819 these two explorers left Tripoli in Libya, intending to travel south to the Niger. By the time they reached Murzuq—the town from which Hornemann had written his last letters—Lyon and Ritchie were out of funds and suffering from fever. Ritchie died that November. Lyon tried to continue the trek, but ventured only a little further south before returning home. The death toll was mounting. In the contest between European explorers and the perils of West Africa, the perils were clearly in the lead.

Clapperton, Denham, and Oudney

Despite the deaths of Hornemann, Park, and Ritchie, Europeans were not willing to give up. In 1822, the government of England, taking up where the African Association had left off, decided to sponsor yet another expedition to locate the mouth of the Niger. Once again, political officials decided, they would send a party from the Mediterranean south across the Sahara. This time, the expedition would include three important leaders: an English army officer named Dixon Denham, and two Scotsmen, Walter Oudney and Hugh Clapperton.

The three proved a volatile mix. Both Oudney and Denham believed themselves to be in charge, and each was shocked to discover that the other disagreed. The two Scotsmen found Denham arrogant, obnoxious, and inexperienced. Denham considered Oudney and Clapperton the "most tiresome companions imaginable."[49] The quarrel between the explorers would last throughout their journey. Except in the direst of situations, the men often did not bother speaking to each other.

Despite the personality conflicts, the travelers got off to a reasonable start. Their pockets full of money and their servants entrusted with thirty-seven camel-loads of trade goods, they left Tripoli in early 1822 in the company of a group of Arab merchants. After spending the summer in and around Murzuq, they continued south that November. Before long they were traveling into territory unseen by any European other than Hornemann.

The going was difficult. The scenery became increasingly bare and dry, and the spaces between oases ever longer. The bones of unfortunate travelers littered the path, stark reminders of the dangers of trekking through the barren Sahara. The three explorers were both repulsed and moved by the skeletons that lay near one oasis. "Those of two women, whose perfect and regular teeth bespoke them young, were particularly shocking,"[50] mused Denham.

As the caravan continued south, conditions grew worse. Dunes rose up with near-vertical slopes sixty feet high. Soft sand slowed the camels' progress and made them stumble. Long-awaited oases proved dry, or their waters salty and unfit to drink. Some of the camels died of thirst and overwork. The travelers began to wonder if they, too, would join the ranks of those whose bones were scattered along the highway.

Lake Chad and Beyond

After six weeks and nearly seven hundred miles of travel, the Europeans noted a gradual greening of the countryside. Early in February 1823, they suddenly came upon the shores of Lake Chad, a large body of water whose existence had been only a rumor to Europeans. Unlike the desert that rose up to the north, the region around the lake was lush and inhabited by flamingos, geese, and other birds. "The sight," wrote Denham, "conveyed to my mind a sensation so gratifying and inspiring, that it would be difficult in language to convey an idea of its force or pleasure."[51]

The travelers were warmly welcomed by the Muslim ruler of the nearby city of Kuka. Denham, Oudney, and Clapperton were taken aback by the reception they received—and by the sophistication of Kukan society. They had half expected a ragtag, subsistence-level culture in which, as Denham put it, the monarch held court "under a tree, surrounded by a few naked slaves."[52] But that was not the case at all. Here in the heart of Africa, the travelers were surprised to see Kuka's well-equipped army, thriving marketplace, and storehouses full of goods ranging from dried fish to muskets.

The friendliness of the people of Kuka allowed the men to refresh themselves for further exploration. Although they had traveled far, their journey was by no means complete. Perhaps the Niger flowed into Lake Chad, or perhaps the elusive river lay somewhere nearby. Denham and his companions would have to find out. The men resolved to use Kuka as a base for further exploration into the wilderness. With luck, they reasoned, one of these smaller expeditions would reach the Niger. Even if they did not, the explorers would visit and describe miles of countryside unknown to Europeans.

Between the spring of 1823 and the summer of 1824, the travelers undertook several journeys into the area surrounding Kuka. Denham, who preferred to travel without his Scottish companions, went on two large-scale treks. On the first, he traveled some distance to the south as part of a slave raid organized by his Muslim hosts. Later, Denham tried to travel around Lake Chad, only to turn back when warfare in the area blocked further progress. "The excursion you wished to make was always dangerous," he was told by an escort provided by the ruler of Kuka. "It is now impracticable."[53]

A ring of palm trees surrounds a desert oasis. Explorers Hugh Clapperton, Dixon Denham, and Walter Oudney followed a path of oases across the Sahara.

Clapperton and Oudney, in the meantime, headed west. Oudney, who had been sick for much of the trip, died not long after leaving Kuka, but Clapperton continued. He eventually reached Sokoto, the capital of the Hausa nation, which lay about five hundred miles west of Kuka.

Clapperton found the journey fascinating and disorienting. The items for sale at one marketplace along the way included French writing paper and English umbrellas, carried overland through the Sahara all the way from the Mediterranean. The ruler of the Hausa was familiar not

 ## Denham's Escape

One of Dixon Denham's expeditions away from Lake Chad nearly resulted in his death. Upon hearing that a group of people from Bornu—the area around Kuka—were planning a raid upon some peoples to the south, Denham quickly saddled up his horse and joined them. The trip, however, was miserable. The heat was appalling and the flies were worse. "My hands and eyes were so swelled," he wrote (quoted in Fergus Fleming's *Barrow's Boys*), "that I could scarcely hold a pen, or see to use one." Moreover, most of his traveling companions resented the fact that he was a European and a Christian.

Dixon Denham nearly lost his life on an expedition away from Lake Chad in 1823.

But the worst of the journey took place during the attack itself. In the battle, Denham was grazed by an arrow, and enemy soldiers shot his horse out from under him. The opposing army might well have killed him as he lay on the ground, but for some reason the soldiers began arguing instead over the distribution of his clothing. While they argued, Denham slid himself beneath the body of another horse and made a successful dash for the safety of a nearby forest.

Still, Denham was not in an enviable position. As Fleming described it, "Naked, [Denham] sped through the trees, scrambling over thorny thickets, plunging through rivers, dodging leopards and venomous serpents, until he finally made his way back to the Bornu army." Even then, he was almost left to die of his wounds and might have died had not a companion come to his assistance. It was a harrowing journey, and unfortunately Denham came away from it with few clear records of the region.

only with England but with the details of British foreign policy as well. Clapperton had expected to find ignorant savages in this remote part of West Africa. He was sobered to realize that the people of this region knew a great deal more about Europe than his own countrymen knew of Africa.

But Sokoto was the farthest Clapperton would go. Sick, exhausted, and informed by the Hausa leader that the Niger was still several hundred miles distant, he returned to Kuka. He and Denham put aside their differences long enough to head home together. They arrived in England in 1825, having failed to see the Niger, let alone to find its mouth. Still, the men had crossed the Sahara, located Lake Chad, and explored miles of the West African interior. Oudney's death notwithstanding, Clapperton and Denham had reason to be proud of their accomplishments.

Clapperton Tries Again

Denham did no more exploration in West Africa, though he did return to the region to take up an administrative position as governor of Sierra Leone. Clapperton, however, had other African adventures in mind. In particular, he still hoped to view the Niger and follow the great river to its mouth. Soon after arriving in London, Clapperton secured government backing to undertake a second voyage into the African interior.

Previously, all major European expeditions into the interior had followed one of two routes. Either the travelers had be-

gun on Africa's western coast, like Park, and worked their way inland, or they had left from the Mediterranean Sea, like Hornemann, and headed south across the Sahara. Clapperton, however, was eager to pioneer a new route. Starting his journey at Badagry, a seaport in modern-day Nigeria, he planned to head north to the River Niger, perhaps beyond.

Clapperton's idea made sense. Badagry was the closest coastal point to Sokoto, the most distant point he had reached on his previous expedition. The trip from Badagry to this part of the Niger would be many miles shorter than the same journey undertaken from Gambia or Libya.

Late in 1825, Clapperton set off from Badagry with about ten fellow European travelers and a handful of African servants and interpreters. Though at first the party had to make its way through dense tropical forest, the countryside soon opened up slightly. Clapperton noted in his journal that the land was "well watered with many fine streams" and found the overall effect to be "quite enchanting."[54] Moreover, he and his companions came to know and appreciate the people of the region. The Yoruba, in particular, struck Clapperton as unfailingly kind and gentle.

But before long, the rigors of the journey began to take their toll. In January 1826, Clapperton's men started to sicken and die. The mosquitoes were as deadly in their own way as were the burning sands and terrible dryness of the desert to the north. By February, Clapperton and his personal servant, an Englishman

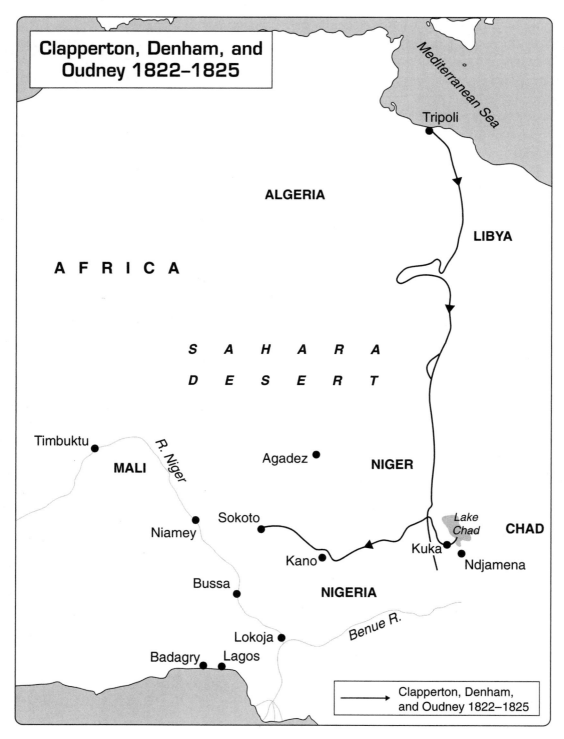

Clapperton, Denham, and
Oudney 1822–1825

ALGERIA

LIBYA

AFRICA

S A H A R A
D E S E R T

Mediterranean Sea

Tripoli

Timbuktu

R. Niger

MALI

Agadez

NIGER

Sokoto

Niamey

Kano

Kuka

Lake
Chad

CHAD

Ndjamena

Bussa

NIGERIA

Benue R.

Lokoja

Badagry   Lagos

Clapperton, Denham,
and Oudney 1822–1825

named Richard Lander, were the only European survivors. Clapperton and Lander continued on struggling northward.

In April the two men reached the Niger at Bussa, the site of Park's death. Clapperton had hoped to set off immediately down the Niger, but the rainy season was coming. After the terrible death toll his group had experienced in the forest, he decided it would be better to wait out the wet weather. He and Lander crossed the river and continued on to Sokoto. By returning to the place he had visited earlier from the north, Clapperton thus completed a two-part crossing of West Africa, making him the first European to do so.

"I Shall Never Recover"

This time Sokoto brought Clapperton nothing but trouble. The Hausa were preparing for a war against a neighboring people, and the arrival of the Europeans was greeted with suspicion. Some charged that the men were spies for the Hausa's enemies. Others thought they were smugglers. The travelers were placed under house arrest and refused permission to leave. Not until March 12, 1827, after several months of waiting, were Clapperton and Lander at last told that they could resume their expedition.

But the news came too late for Clapperton. That very evening he came down with a severe case of dysentery, which he believed he had contracted from lying on soft, wet soil some time earlier. "I shall never recover,"[55] he told Lander—and he

A Yoruba ruler sits on a throne decorated with elephant tusks. Hugh Clapperton considered the Yoruba people to be kind and gentle.

never did. During the next month, his condition worsened. He grew thinner and weaker; his sleep became fitful and his breathing difficult. In mid-April, after instructing Lander to take the best possible care of the expedition's papers and journals, Clapperton died.

The death left Lander in a difficult situation. Clapperton was the head of the expedition, the one who had made all the decisions. Lander lacked experience,

Despite his fears, Lander resolved to carry on with the expedition. Leaving Sokoto, he headed south toward the Niger. There he hoped to commandeer a canoe and set off down the river until he arrived at its mouth. He might have done it, too, but as he made his way south, he learned that warfare was raging along the lower stretches of the river. The people he encountered all tried to dissuade him from his adventure, and by the time Lander reached the Niger, he was ready to accept their advice. He headed back to Badagry and eventually sailed for home, taking with him Clapperton's journal, a journal of his own, and a suitcase full of miscellaneous notes about the trip.

Another Expedition

Lander returned from his remarkable solo journey with something less tangible, too: a burning desire to complete the quest Clapperton had begun. Like Clapperton, Lander had become enchanted by Africa and the excitement of discovery. Despite the terrible hardships he had endured while traveling to and from Sokoto, he yearned to go back. "There was a charm in the very sound of Africa," he wrote, "that always made my heart flutter on hearing it mentioned."[57] He immediately began to lobby the English government to appoint him head of another expedition to the River Niger.

By any standard, Lander was an unlikely expedition leader. In nineteenth-century England, all that mattered was breeding and education, and Lander had

Clapperton died of dysentery during his 1827 expedition to find the mouth of the Niger.

authority, and knowledge. He was a servant, not an explorer, and he had only a rudimentary ability to navigate across unknown lands. "[I] could not help being deeply affected with my lonesome and dangerous situation," Lander wrote. "I felt, indeed, as if I stood alone in the world, and earnestly wished that I had been laid by the side of my dear master."[56]

neither. But John Barrow, the English politician who oversaw the British program of exploration at the time, nevertheless accepted Lander's proposal. True, Barrow offered little financial support and expected less in the way of results. Still, he reasoned that an investment of a few hundred pounds might prove worthwhile. "With a bundle of beads and bafts [a kind of fabric] and other trinkets," Barrow wrote dismissively, "we could land him somewhere around Bonny [a West African river] and let him find his way."[58]

Lander lost no time preparing for his expedition. Enlisting the help of his brother John, Lander arrived in Badagry in March 1830. The two men quickly gathered provisions and hired a few African servants and interpreters. Then they headed into the wilderness. Staying surprisingly healthy, given the fevers that had struck down Clapperton, Oudney, Hornemann, and practically all of Mungo Park's traveling companions, the men made good time. By June, they had reached Bussa and the Niger.

Richard Lander and the Widow Zuma

Along their way north to the River Niger, Hugh Clapperton and Richard Lander encountered an African woman known as the Widow Zuma. This woman was among the wealthiest people in the community—"vastly rich," Lander called her, quoted in Margery Perham and J. Simmons's *African Discovery*—and she was passionately eager to get to know the two explorers. In particular, she had her eyes on Lander, whom she hoped would consent to settle in her town and marry her.

Lander had absolutely no interest in the widow. He took pains in his journal to describe her as old and fat, though he admitted that she had "large, full, and certainly beautiful eyes" and might have been pretty "in her younger years." Shy and easily embarrassed, though, he had trouble dealing with the widow's obvious interest. He was uncomfortable refusing the various presents she sent him or turning her away when she came to the door of the home where they were staying. Nor did it help that Clapperton found the whole thing enormously funny. As Lander put it, Clapperton "did his utmost to inflame the lady's passion, by passing a thousand unmeaning compliments on the regularity of my features, and the handsomeness of my person."

Lander finally summoned the courage to tell the widow that he could not settle in her town. That was all right with her, the woman told him. "[I will] follow you to whichever part of the world you may be inclined to lead me to," she explained. To this, Lander at last told her point-blank that he had no interest in marrying her and never would. He expected tears and anger; instead, the woman simply turned her attentions elsewhere—to Clapperton. Perhaps not surprisingly, the two explorers soon moved on.

Here, though, their expedition stalled. Their biggest problem was acquiring a canoe on the limited budget Barrow had given Lander. The brothers had few trade goods to offer other than needles and cloth, neither of which proved to be in high demand in this part of West Africa. Thus, they had no way of persuading any African to give up his canoe to them. At first their problem was merely annoying, but as the summer progressed and their remaining supplies dwindled, the brothers grew more and more concerned. Without a canoe, their expedition was at an end.

In mid-September, the brothers' luck changed. Whether by barter or outright theft—sources differ—they managed to obtain two boats. Both of these canoes were small and leaky and scarcely adequate for the trip. The men had little choice, however. Accompanied by a team of African paddlers, the brothers quickly packed up and set out down the Niger.

Downstream

In many ways, the trip was a nightmare. The canoes leaked so badly that the men were forced to bail almost constantly. As they traveled downstream, the brothers tried desperately to trade their boats for something more suitable. Again and again, they met people who claimed to have good boats available for sale or trade, but none of these assertions came to anything. "They have played with us as if we were great dolls," fumed John

Lander. "Why this double dealing, this deceit, this chicanery?"[59]

At last the brothers made a trade, exchanging their two leaky boats—along with a quantity of needles—for a single canoe they had been assured was both roomy and in good condition. In fact, it was neither. The new canoe was clearly unworthy of the price, and the brothers were tempted to bargain for a better deal. But in the end, they had no wish to spend countless hours involved in negotiation that might well accomplish nothing. The brothers instead transferred their equipment into the new craft and continued on their way, still bailing as they went. They did gain a measure of revenge, however, by stealing several good paddles from the man who had engineered the trade.

The river presented many other obstacles. At one point, a herd of hippopotamuses came storming into the river. The men tried to shoot them, but the noise only stirred the great beasts into a panic. The paddlers "trembled with fear and apprehension," Richard Lander reported, "and absolutely wept aloud."[60] When the canoe at last managed to thread a path through the massive herd, a storm broke and nearly swamped the leaky vessel. Great waves rose up, the winds howled, and the canoe, suddenly uncontrollable, was swept downstream at a furious rate. The travelers barely managed to survive the harrowing experience.

Nevertheless, the men were making significant progress. This part of the river was wholly unknown to European travelers, and every mile brought the

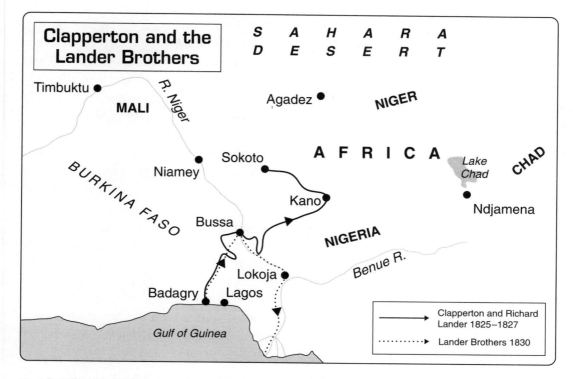

Clapperton and the Lander Brothers

Clapperton and Richard Lander 1825–1827
Lander Brothers 1830

Landers new information about the lands and peoples of the region. They charted the landscape and noted the twists and turns of the river as it traveled steadily southeast. They noted the location of villages and tributaries, or smaller rivers that joined the flow of the Niger. It became increasingly clear that the Niger was carrying them back to the Atlantic—not to Lake Chad, the Zaire River, or some impenetrable swamp in the center of the continent. Slowly, the Landers were unraveling one of the great mysteries of African geography.

Final Difficulties

In late October, the men saw a seagull and knew they were getting close to the ocean at last. European trade goods, brought inland from the Nigerian coast, began to appear along the sides of the river. The travelers were cheered to see familiar items such as barrels and iron bars of European manufacture. The signs of the nearby sea and of distant Europe evoked a sense of homesickness in the men. They increased their pace, hoping that soon they would be boarding a freighter headed for England.

But their adventure was not yet done. On November 4, 1830, the explorers were suddenly attacked by a large group of men in canoes. Armed with cannons, these men rammed and sank the Landers' canoe, robbed the travelers of almost all their possessions, and took the entire group as prisoners. They brought the Europeans by canoe into the Niger delta, a network of small rivers and streams, and informed them that they were being held for ransom. The Landers' captors were convinced that the skipper of an English vessel in the harbor downstream would pay dearly to reclaim his fellow countrymen.

The brothers, however, knew this was unlikely. The price demanded by their captors—twenty slaves or the equivalent in other goods—seemed impossibly high. They were not surprised when the captain flatly refused to pay the ransom. Desperate, Richard Lander assured the captain that the British government would reimburse him (though Lander probably knew this was an empty promise). This argument had no effect either; the

skipper again turned down the request.

But luck, once again, was with the Lander brothers. Half the ship's crew had recently died of fever, leaving the captain in need of able seamen. When he realized that the brothers might be able to help him sail the ship, he rethought his position. Promising the brothers' captors that he would pay the ransom after all, the captain took the explorers aboard. Then, before the Africans could react, he hurried from the harbor and steered into the open ocean. He carried the Landers to an offshore island several weeks' journey from the Niger. From there the brothers boarded a ship to Brazil, and once in South America they found a ship that would take them home. They reached England in June 1831.

Explorers and Fashion

The question of what to wear was important to European explorers of West Africa during the nineteenth century. Some explorers argued that Western travelers in the region ought to dress just as the natives did, or as close as possible. Using standard European clothing, remarked one expert, quoted in Fergus Fleming's *Barrow's Boys,* "will at any rate expose [European travelers] to much unnecessary annoyance, even supposing it should not endanger their personal safety." Friedrich Hornemann was a passionate advocate of this approach.

But others vehemently disagreed. Dixon Denham, for instance, argued that such disguises were unnecessary, silly, and counterproductive. "[We] had determined to travel in our real character as Britons and Christians," he reported, also quoted in Fleming's book. In his eyes, the English clothing impressed the locals and discouraged them from staging attacks. "Our reception," he stated, "would have been less friendly had we assumed a character that could at best have been ill-supported. In trying to make ourselves appear as Mussulmans [Muslims], we should have been set down as real imposters." In the end, some expeditions chose one strategy; others adopted the other.

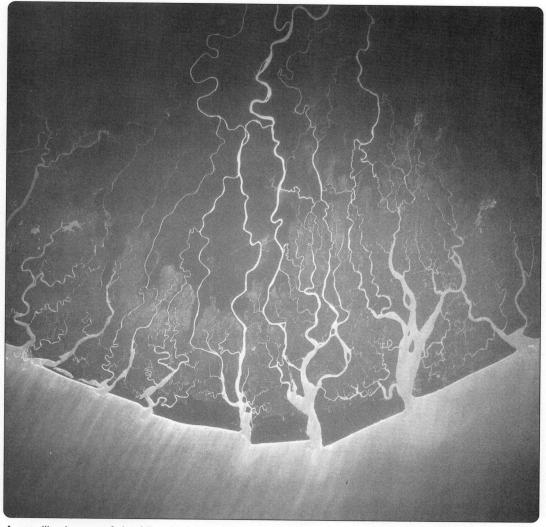

A satellite image of the Niger's delta shows the river flowing south into the Atlantic Ocean at the Gulf of Guinea.

They had done well. The brothers had traveled to the end of the Niger and demonstrated that it did indeed pour into the Atlantic. They had discovered that the seemingly insignificant streams and tidal estuaries along the Nigerian coast were actually the great delta of one of the mightiest of all rivers. And they had filled in some of the largest blank spaces on the European map of West Africa. The riddles of West Africa were rapidly being solved, and the Lander brothers, like Clapperton, Denham, and Oudney before them, had played an essential role in finding the solutions.

CHAPTER FIVE

In Search of Timbuktu

The quest to find the mouth of the River Niger was the task that most intrigued European adventurers of the early 1800s. But farther upstream, the Niger held a second mystery as well: the fabled city of Timbuktu, once the capital of the great Mali Empire. According to the rumors heard by Europeans along the West African coast, the city was magnificent beyond all comprehension. Those who heard the tales generally accepted them as fact. The ruler of the city, wrote one English merchant in 1809, was so rich that even "the massive bolts in his different palaces were of pure gold."[61]

Europeans longed to see a city of such magnificence, and a few of the travelers who set out to reach the Niger had dreams of visiting Timbuktu as well. During his first expedition, for example, Park had hoped to journey on to the city after arriving at the Niger. Similarly, Clapperton made inquiries about Timbuktu on his travels west from Lake Chad. But getting to the city proved extraordinarily difficult. Its exact location was uncertain, the best route to it unknown. By the early 1800s, West Africans reported, the region around the city had become dangerous, its fringes inhabited largely

by warlike peoples who refused to let strangers pass unimpeded.

As a result, the city remained completely unknown to Europeans. Except for Mungo Park and a handful of companions, who had floated by it during their disastrous second expedition, no European had seen the city. And of course Park and his men had left no records of their trip. To Europeans of the early nineteenth century, then, Timbuktu was a blank spot on the map of Africa— and an uncommonly intriguing one. Beginning in the 1820s, even as other explorers investigated the course of the Niger further downstream, a series of adventurers tried to make their way to the legendary city of gold.

Gordon Laing

The first of these men was Gordon Laing. Like Clapperton, Oudney, and Park, Laing was Scottish; like Denham, he was an officer in the British army. Those who knew Laing generally agreed that he was intelligent and brave. They also agreed, however, that Laing was self-important, overly ambitious, and hard to get along with. As a young officer, Laing had been posted to Tripoli on Libya's Mediterranean shores. There Laing became deeply intrigued by Africa and the remaining riddles of African geography.

In 1822 the British government chose Laing to carry out a short expedition in Sierra Leone, mainly to establish trading contacts between Britain and the people of the interior. Laing suspected that the source of the Niger lay within the region through which he was traveling, and the people he met confirmed his theory. Because of hostilities in the area, Laing was unable to visit the exact spot where the Niger began. But he came close enough to realize that the Niger could not possibly flow into the Nile. Southern Egypt, he pointed out, was at a higher elevation than the land in this part of West Africa—and water never flowed uphill.

Laing's conclusions were accepted by some and ignored by others. Regardless, his experiences made him eager to learn more. He applied to his superiors to undertake another journey, this one beginning in Sierra Leone and continuing east

A sign in Morocco indicates that it is a fifty-two-day journey by camel to the city of Tombouctou (Timbuktu). In the 1800s Europeans were fascinated by the fabled city.

until he reached the Niger closer to Timbuktu. Turned down largely because of his youth and inexperience, Laing resolved to try again. "I have," he explained, "a strong desire to penetrate into the interior of Africa."[62]

The word *desire* was an understatement; *obsession* might have been a better choice. Before long, arranging a journey

British soldier Gordon Laing was obsessed with finding the city of Timbuktu.

to Timbuktu was almost constantly on Laing's mind. "I am so wrapt up in the success of this enterprise," he wrote at one point, "that I think of nothing else all day and dream of nothing else all night."[63] He wrote letters to anyone in authority, hoping to win support for a trip to the great city. He volunteered to forgo a salary if necessary, and he studied the works of previous explorers so he would be ready if and when the time came.

Laing also acted as though Timbuktu and the Niger somehow belonged to him. Before long he was insisting that only he was qualified to make a trek to the region. He dismissed the work of Clapperton and Denham as being of no value, since his Sierra Leone expedition had already demonstrated that the Niger could not join the Nile. When he heard that Clapperton was being sponsored for a second Niger expedition, Laing became furious. "Clapperton may as well have stayed at home," he fumed. "[This journey] is destined for me. . . . If I do not visit [Timbuktu] the world will forever remain in ignorance of that place."[64]

Under other circumstances, Laing's temper and intensity might have kept government officials from sending him into the unknown. But these were not ordinary times. Although England had once been the only European country with an interest in exploring the West African interior, that was no longer the case. Other countries were beginning to study the region and mount expeditions of their own. A French geographical society had even offered a reward to the first explorer who

Tennyson and Timbuktu

In 1828–1829, Cambridge University in England held its annual poetry contest. The topic the contest organizers chose was Timbuktu, an indication of the hold the supposedly great city had on the imaginations of Europeans at the time. The contest was won by a young college student named Alfred Tennyson, later to be a famous poet. Tennyson's winning entry lamented that the actual characteristics of a place might prove far less interesting than the romantic notions people had held before. The poem is quoted on the University of South Carolina Libraries Web site.

English poet Alfred Tennyson won a poetry contest on the topic of Timbuktu in 1829.

Oh City! oh latest Throne! where I was rais'd
To be a mystery of loveliness
Unto all eyes, the time is well-nigh come
When I must render up this glorious home
To keen *Discovery:* soon yon brilliant towers
Shall darken with the waving of her wand:
Darken, and shrink and shiver into huts,
Black specks amid a waste of dreary sand,
Low-built, mud-wall'd, Barbarian settlements.
How chang'd this fair City!

traveled to Timbuktu and back, and several French adventurers were considering making the trek themselves.

This was unwelcome news to the English. To have some other nation claim the honor of being first to Timbuktu would be a blow to Britain's national pride.

Moreover, it would put Britain at a disadvantage in establishing commercial ties with the fabulously wealthy people of the city. Laing might not have been the wisest choice to venture toward Timbuktu, but he was available, he was eager, and time was short. In 1825, having obtained official sponsorship of his proposed journey, Laing returned to Tripoli and started on his adventure.

Across the Sahara

Laing's plans were grand. In a period of just six months, he assured doubtful officials, he would reach the Niger, visit Timbuktu and find the river's end. To fit all this into the brief time frame, Laing planned to head out across the Sahara along a new route, one that would take him along a rough diagonal southwest from Tripoli. There had been a caravan track along this route, Laing knew, and he meant to follow it. In July 1825, Laing and a few fellow travelers set out from Tripoli for the Saharan city of Ghadames, a trading center in modern-day Libya.

Six months was a woeful underestimate. Forced to detour by a war among local peoples, Laing and his party did not reach Ghadames until mid-September, and it was November by the time they managed to press on. By January 1826, six months after leaving Tripoli, Laing had gotten no further than the northern Sahara community of In Salah in present-day Algeria. By this time, Laing had anticipated striding in triumph onto a British ship at the mouth of the Niger, his notebooks bulging with all possible information about Timbuktu and the course of the mighty river. In truth, however, he had barely traveled halfway to the city.

Conditions only got worse. Temperatures reached 120 degrees Fahrenheit in the shade. Water holes dried up; food supplies ran low. But Laing scarcely seemed to mind. Indeed, he used the hardships as examples of his courage and strength. He took pride in pointing out his ability to withstand the appalling heat of the desert. Any true adventurer, he insisted, would prefer the obscure, dangerous pathway he had chosen to the better known trail followed by Clapperton and Denham. Their route, he asserted disdainfully, was "a regular trading road . . . along which a child might travel."[65]

Just how dangerous Laing's route was, he would shortly find out. A few weeks after leaving In Salah, his caravan was besieged by bandits wielding swords. In the attack Laing suffered severe cuts to his neck, temple, leg, and arm. One of his hands was nearly sliced off. Somehow he survived, only to catch the plague shortly afterward. But even these disasters failed to deter him from his mission. Single-minded as ever and fearful that Clapperton would reach Timbuktu before him, he continued south.

In August 1826, more than a year after leaving Tripoli, Laing staggered into Timbuktu—the first Westerner known to have set eyes on the city. At first he was tolerated by the residents of the city. But over the next few weeks the city's rulers grew suspicious of Laing's intentions. Rumors began to spread that he was not simply a harmless, injured eccentric, but a spy sent out by Britain to begin the process of colonizing all of

West Africa. After a little more than a month in the city, Laing was summoned before the local sultan and told to leave town immediately.

Instead of continuing down the Niger as originally planned, Laing decided to head north. He quickly joined a caravan and began the long journey back across the Sahara. Three days into the journey raiders, possibly acting under orders from a local tribal leader, attacked and killed Laing. His papers were destroyed, and his fate remained unknown to the wider world for many months. A later explorer learned details of Laing's trip.

In addition, one relic of Laing's epic journey survived: a letter he had written and sent back across the desert shortly after his arrival in Timbuktu. That letter, though brief, was tantalizing. "In every respect except in size," Laing wrote, "[Timbuktu] has completely met my expectations."[66]

René-Auguste Caillié

The next man to try for Timbuktu was in many ways as unlike Laing as could be imagined. Laing was a military officer; René-Auguste Caillié, in contrast,

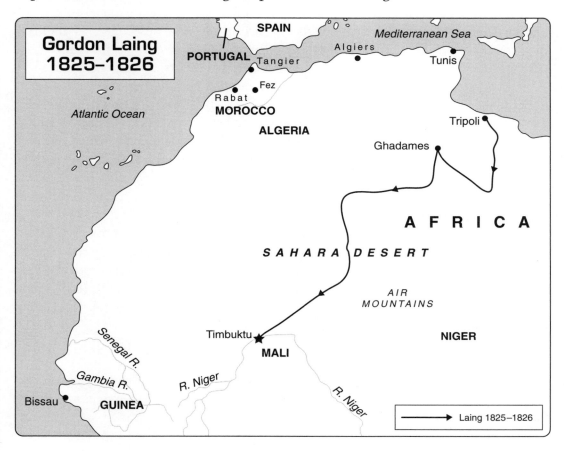

Gordon Laing 1825–1826

SPAIN
Mediterranean Sea
Algiers
Tunis
PORTUGAL
Tangier
Fez
Rabat
MOROCCO
Atlantic Ocean
ALGERIA
Tripoli
Ghadames
AFRICA
SAHARA DESERT
AIR MOUNTAINS
NIGER
Timbuktu
MALI
Senegal R.
Gambia R.
R. Niger
R. Niger
Bissau
GUINEA
Laing 1825–1826

was a poorly educated man who had held a succession of dead-end jobs. Laing was a comfortable member of the ruling class; Caillié was the son of a thief. Laing's expedition was backed by the power and money of England; Caillié had no assistance from his government. And Laing was British, whereas Caillié was French. In these respects, the two men had little in common.

But Caillié and Laing did share one important characteristic: an obsession with Africa. In Caillié's case, the yen to explore had begun early. As a boy, he had read the novel *Robinson Crusoe,* about a castaway on a desert island. This novel had sparked in him a desire for adventure. As a youth, he sought an appropriate place to explore and found one. "The map of Africa," he reflected, "in which I saw scarcely any but countries marked as desert or unknown, excited my attention more than any other."[67] Orphaned young and with no particular ties to his native country, Caillié soon began looking for passage to Africa. At the age of sixteen, he found it: He was hired as a servant by a military officer bound for Senegal.

Africa was every bit as wonderful as Caillié had hoped. Over the next few years, he joined several expeditions into the interior near Senegal. During most of these journeys, he and his companions suffered horribly from heat and exhaustion. "My eyes were hollow," he wrote of his experiences on one expedition. "My tongue hung out of my mouth . . . [I] had not even the strength to eat."[68]

But still, like Laing, he was not interested in returning to an easier life in Europe. Indeed, when Caillié heard of the prize the French were awarding to the first traveler to reach Timbuktu he reacted much like Laing. "Dead or alive," he vowed, "the prize shall be mine."[69]

Caillié knew that he had no chance of gathering any official support for this trek. He was too poor, too obscure, too inexperienced. Accordingly, he made plans of his own. First he worked at a series of odd jobs as, among other things, a servant, cook, and farm manager—whatever would earn him the money he would need to pay for the trip. Through careful savings, he eventually had two thousand francs. With this money, he bought presents, trade goods, and medicines for the long trip ahead.

Next, he planned his disguise. Because he had experienced firsthand the hostility Christian travelers in Africa received from some Muslims, Caillie decided to pass himself off as a Muslim—much as Friedrich Hornemann had done more than twenty years earlier. For nine months, Caillié lived among a group of Muslims in Senegal. During this time he learned the rudiments of their language and their customs. In March 1827 he was ready to begin his dangerous journey.

The Journey East
Caillié first traveled to a large river on the border between Senegal and Sierra Leone. This region was a common gathering place for travelers, and Caillié quickly

A herd of antelope in Senegal grazes beneath baobab trees. As a teenager, René-Auguste Caillié explored the West African interior near Senegal.

joined a caravan of Muslims heading east. To explain his incomplete knowledge of Muslim cultures, languages, and religious matters, he told his fellow travelers that he was an Egyptian by birth. As a young boy, he added, he had been captured by the French and raised in Europe without much knowledge of his true religious heritage. Now he was returning home. The cover story was wildly successful. "I said prayers with my new friends," Caillié recalled, "after

which they received me as a true Musulman [Muslim]."[70]

The travelers made good time. By June they had reached the Niger at Kurasso, less than a hundred miles from the river's source. By August, now traveling with a different caravan, Caillié had reached the town of Tieme. There, however, he came down with malaria, and then a case of scurvy, a disease caused by a lack of fresh food. "The roof of my mouth became quite bare," Caillié wrote, describing his

Caillié disguised himself as a Muslim trader while journeying across the Sahara.

troubles. "My teeth seemed ready to drop out of their sockets . . . I was more than a fortnight [two weeks] without sleep."[71] To make matters worse, he developed a terrible sore on his foot.

Continuing was impossible. Indeed, Caillié lay near death for several weeks. He probably would not have survived without the expert nursing care provided him by an elderly resident of the town. Not until January 1828 was he in any condition to move on. But like Laing, he never considered going back to Sierra Leone. "I would rather have died on the road," he wrote afterward, "than have returned without making more important discoveries."[72] Sick, weary, and low

on supplies, Caillié nevertheless continued his overland journey, heading always in the direction of Timbuktu.

In March, Caillié reached a tributary of the Niger and joined a group heading downstream aboard an enormous canoe. Despite its size, the vessel traveled with agonizing slowness, and Caillié suffered from the sun, heat, and fever. Matters grew worse as the canoe approached Timbuktu. Though no one had penetrated his disguise, Caillie's pale skin was impossible to hide. Friendly Africans aboard the canoe warned that marauding bandits might mistake him for a hated European and suggested that he conceal himself under a pile of mats as the vessel floated the last few dozen miles. Although the hiding place was hot and uncomfortable, Caillié took their advice.

"An Indescribable Satisfaction"

On April 20, 1828, more than a year after he had set out from Sierra Leone, Caillié achieved his dream. That evening, he walked into the legendary city of Tim-

buktu. At last he had reached the destination he had longed to visit for so many years. "I experienced an indescribable satisfaction," he wrote. "With what gratitude did I return thanks to Heaven, for the happy result which attended my enterprise!"[73]

As Caillié looked around him, however, his excitement dwindled. Timbuktu, he discovered, was not at all a great city of gold as generations of Europeans had believed. There was little sign of wealth

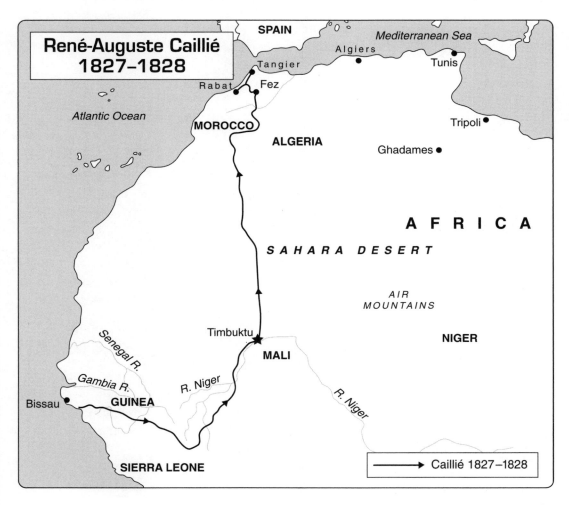

or even of ordinary prosperity. The streets were uncrowded, the population small, the buildings low and drab. "The city presented, at first view, nothing but a mass of ill-looking houses, built of earth," Caillié wrote. "Nothing was to be seen in all directions but immense planes of quicksand. . . . All nature wore a dreary aspect, and the most profound silence prevailed."[74]

Caillié soon concluded that his initial impression was correct. There were no magnificent palaces, no fine houses of worship. Timbuktu had little to recommend itself; indeed, Caillié had seen more impressive towns elsewhere along his route. Disappointed, he remained in the city for only two weeks. During this time, he made inquiries about the history of the city and described the people and layout of Timbuktu as thoroughly as he could.

Caillié's route home was no easier than his route to Timbuktu. Instead of going back to the west coast, he decided to travel northward with a large caravan of Muslims. The desert, however, nearly did him in. Like every other explorer who had crossed the Sahara, Caillié suffered terribly from heat, exhaustion, and most of all thirst. At last, in September, after a horrible journey of three months and well over one thousand miles, he reached the Moroccan city of Tangier. From there he

 ## Robert Adams

The great race for Timbuktu, ironically enough, may have been lost by both the English and the French long before it actually began. From time to time throughout the 1700s and 1800s, European or American ships were wrecked somewhere along the western coast of Africa. Some of the sailors who survived were taken prisoner by local African peoples; many were sold into slavery, at least temporarily. A few of these slaves who later won their freedom wrote about their travels (or had them ghostwritten) and published them in response to a burgeoning interest in travel literature during the time. Today many of the details of these stories are open to question, but the core of the tales do seem more or less accurate.

One such book was the 1816 narrative of an American sailor named Robert Adams, who had been shipwrecked off the West African coast. According to the University of South Carolina Libraries Web site, Adams said that he had been held as a slave for three years by the "Arabs of the Great Desert [the Sahara]." Moreover, Adams claimed to have spent six months of that time in Timbuktu—or "Tomboctoo," as he called it—before eventually making his way to England. If his account can be believed—and that is open to debate—Adams, not Gordon Laing or René Caillié, was the first Westerner to set foot in Timbuktu during modern times, and the first to make his way back as well.

made his way back to France. He was home.

But now Caillié suffered the greatest of indignities. After everything he had been through, he found to his dismay that his story was not universally accepted. The English were particularly vocal: John Barrow called Caillié a fraud. Even Caillié's countrymen were not completely convinced that he had reached Timbuktu. The payment of his reward, in fact, was delayed until a special commission could look into allegations that he had invented the whole story. "These unjust attacks," mourned Caillié, "have affected me more deeply than all the hardships . . . I have encountered in the interior of Africa."[75]

Caillié's story *was* hard to believe. He had traveled alone, so there was no one to corroborate his tale; he had traveled in disguise, so he could not take consistent compass readings or

Drawn by Caillié in 1828, this illustration of Timbuktu contradicts Gordon Laing's description of the city. Most Europeans dismissed Caillié's accounts as fiction.

otherwise prove where he had been. Moreover, the information he brought back to Europe contradicted everything people thought they knew about Timbuktu. It also contradicted Laing's last letter, in which he wrote that Timbuktu had met his expectations. Today it is believed that Laing, ever the self-promoter, lied in order to whet people's appetite for a forthcoming book about his travels. But in a contest between the word of the military man Laing and that of the obscure Caillié, it was reasonable that many observers would side with the former.

The matter, in any case, was not quickly resolved. Over the next few years several other European explorers set out to investigate Timbuktu for themselves, but none succeeded. Some were forced to turn back; others died along the way. It would be more than twenty years before another explorer would visit Timbuktu and establish, once and for all, the truth of Caillié's observations.

Heinrich Barth

By 1850 European understanding of the West African interior was far greater than it had been only fifty or sixty years earlier. Mungo Park had established the direction of the River Niger; Gordon Laing had identified its source, and the Lander brothers its mouth. Hugh Clapperton and Dixon Denham had filled in hundreds of square miles on the map of the continent. René-Auguste Caillié had wandered over two thousand miles across previously uncharted stretches of the region. And a host of lesser-known adventurers had visited other areas of West Africa's tropical forest, savanna, and desert. Still, plenty of unknown territory remained.

In 1850 the English government appointed an explorer named James Richardson to head up yet another expedition to the still-unknown parts of West Africa. Richardson's expedition had several purposes beyond simple geographic discovery. One was the hope of establishing commercial ties with the unknown peoples of remotest West Africa. Another was an attempt to eliminate the slave trade, which, though banned throughout Europe, was still practiced by Arab merchants in the region. A third was the desire to make a scientific study of the lands and peoples of the region.

It was a huge undertaking, and Richardson knew he would need help. He received it in the form of a German scientist named Heinrich Barth. Trained in archaeology and geography, Barth was an experienced explorer who had already made a trek along Africa's Mediterranean coast. Like many previous explorers of West Africa, he was deeply intrigued by the continent and its peoples. In Mediterranean towns, he had sought out travelers from regions to the south and inquired about their countries. Now, with Richardson, Barth would finally have the chance to investigate the region for himself.

At first Barth chafed under Richardson's leadership. Richardson's deepest interests in the adventure involved commerce and the abolition of the slave trade; pure geographic discovery and scientific knowledge were secondary. In contrast, Barth thought that scientific and geographic understanding should be the centerpiece of the journey. Perhaps in part because of this disagreement, or perhaps simply because their personalities were quite different, Richardson and Barth quickly took a strong dislike to each other. As they traveled south from Tripoli into the great Sahara, they kept their distance from each other as much as possible, even setting up different overnight camps whenever they could.

The antipathy between the men worked in Barth's favor in at least one way. Reluctant to spend much time with a man he resented, Richardson decided that the two should split up whenever possible. Consequently, Barth was able to undertake several mini-expeditions of his own as the men traveled south.

Abolition and the Slave Trade

The West African slave trade had gone on for many years before the arrival of the Portuguese, and it continued for quite some time after European nations no longer—officially, at least—participated in it. In the late 1700s, the people of several European nations, including England, began to question the morality of the slave trade and of slavery itself. In the early 1800s, a number of these countries formally banned the ownership, sale, and purchase of slaves. (Even the United States forbade its citizens to bring new African captives into the country or to purchase slaves carried in by others, though this law was not always well enforced.) By the 1820s, most European powers were no longer involved in slave trading.

But mere lack of involvement was not enough. Some of these nations—England among them—decided it was their responsibility to stop the African slave trade. Recognizing that it would be unrealistic to ask longtime slave traders to give up their livelihoods simply on moral grounds, the leaders of these nations decided instead to see if they could develop other commercial possibilities to take the place of the slave trafficking. This goal led to several expeditions during the nineteenth century, including that of James Richardson and Heinrich Barth.

This illustration depicts a group of slaves rescued near Madagascar by the British navy in 1883, long after slavery was made illegal throughout Europe.

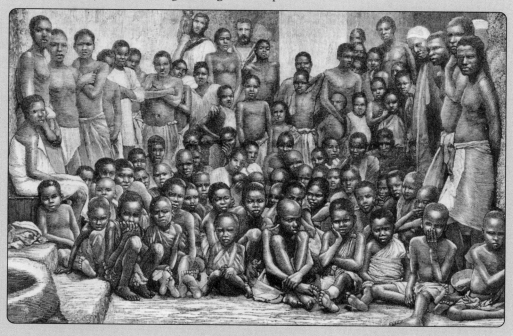

He was delighted to spend his hours investigating the science and geography of West Africa while leaving the commercial issues to his superior. Indeed, Barth might have been content to conclude the journey in just this way. But in March 1851, just a year after the travelers had set out, Richardson died of disease, leaving Barth in charge of the expedition.

Heinrich Barth spent five years in the West African interior to establish commercial ties and describe places previously unknown to Europeans.

The Last Great Expedition

Leading the expedition was a grand opportunity for Barth, and he took full advantage of it. Over the next four years he crisscrossed the deserts and savannas of West Africa, investigating dozens of places little known to Europeans and describing them with great care and insight. Again and again, Barth brought his analytical skills, innate curiosity, and scientific training to bear on his observations of the lands and peoples of the region. When he returned to Europe in 1855, after five years of wandering in some of the world's most remote areas, it took him five full volumes to describe his discoveries and adventures.

His achievements were indeed remarkable. Barth became probably the first European to visit the ancient trading city of Agadez in present-day Niger. Later, he explored large stretches of unknown territory around Lake Chad and made important discoveries about the river system in that region. He described African customs, systems of government, and cultures with which no European was familiar. Given six more months in one region, he boasted, he would have become "fully master of the language with all its finest peculiarities,"[76] and no one who knew him doubted his words.

Barth's adventures were also dramatic. Near Ghat, a trading city in the Sahara, Barth decided to try to climb a local mountain, an adventure previously unattempted by a European. He reached the summit of the mountain without much difficulty but ran out of water on the

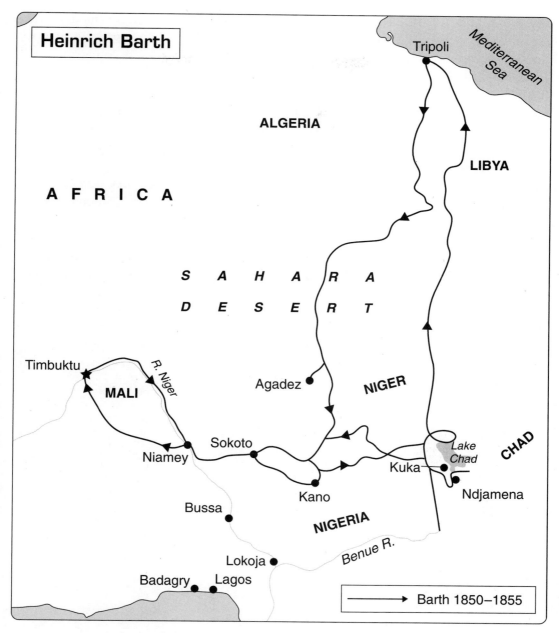

Heinrich Barth

Tripoli

Mediterranean Sea

ALGERIA

LIBYA

A F R I C A

S A H A R A

D E S E R T

Timbuktu

R. Niger

MALI

Agadez

NIGER

Sokoto

Niamey

Lake Chad

Kuka

CHAD

Kano

Ndjamena

Bussa

NIGERIA

Lokoja

Benue R.

Badagry

Lagos

Barth 1850–1855

way back down. Suffering from thirst and exhaustion, he cut open one of his veins and drank some of his blood to quench his thirst. That decision, along with the unexpected assistance of an African passerby, saved his life. Later, he survived robbers, malaria, and an episode in which he was taken prisoner by a king.

Barth's greatest work, however, involved the River Niger and Timbuktu—

the two places where European exploration had concentrated so significantly during the previous sixty years. In late 1852, eager to visit Timbuktu for himself, Barth began to head slowly west from Lake Chad. Before long he was traveling along stretches of the Niger, "the exploration of which," Barth noted solemnly, "has cost the sacrifice of so many lives."[77] In September 1853 he reached Timbuktu and entered the gates of the city.

Barth stayed in the area for seven months, learning what he could about the city and its inhabitants and taking exhaustive notes on both. His thorough description made it abundantly clear that Caillié's impressions were indeed accurate. Timbuktu was no longer a great trading community, as Europeans had believed for generations, but a poor and unimpressive city with little to offer. By the time Barth had published his observations, no European could believe any longer in a still-powerful, still-wealthy Timbuktu.

Barth had settled the question of Timbuktu once and for all. But he had done much, much more. The time he had spent in West Africa was unrivaled by the efforts of any previous explorer; the degree of curiosity and detail he had brought to his assignment was likewise unequaled. As historian Piers Pennington sums up, "No one before him had accomplished so much."[78] Nor would anyone again undertake quite the same adventure. There was no need. Barth's work, from Timbuktu and the River Niger to Lake Chad and beyond, had cleared up most of the remaining mysteries of West African geography.

CONCLUSION

The Effects of Exploration

The expedition of Heinrich Barth did not entirely put an end to West African exploration. In the years that followed his return to Europe, explorers continued to arrive in Ghana, Senegal, Mali, and other parts of the region. But these were primarily small-scale expeditions, concerned with scouting out a particular town, investigating a river, or establishing commercial ties. Some of these expeditions simply followed in the footsteps of earlier adventurers and took survey readings, thus fixing various points more accurately on the West African map.

Other travelers to West Africa increasingly opted for a scientific or anthropological approach. Their concern was not so much the location of West African cities and natural features, but the plants, animals, and human cultures of the area. During the 1890s, for example, English explorer Mary Kingsley made two voyages to Cameroon and elsewhere in West Africa. While she undoubtedly saw places unvisited by any previous European, her main interest was in getting to know the people of the lands through which she traveled. The book she wrote on her experiences is full of details about foods, tools, music, and other aspects of local cultures. It remains an informative, engaging, and largely respectful account of the West African cultures during the 1890s.

But most of the Europeans who went to West Africa during Kingsley's time and afterward were not interested in the people; nor were they interested in the geography. Instead, they were interested in power. The years of the late nineteenth and early twentieth centuries were the years of the so-called Scramble for Africa—a time when the great European nations struggled with one another to carve out colonies all through the African continent.

To a degree, the process of colonization had been going on in West Africa for years. Portuguese traders—and later the English, French, and Dutch—had all established spheres of influence around various African ports. As explorers ventured inland, too, their countries took a

Members of the Fang tribe transport English explorer Mary Kingsley (sitting behind flag) in a canoe. Kingsley traveled throughout West Africa during the 1890s.

proprietary interest in the areas through which they traveled. But in the 1880s, the process grew both more formal and more immediate. With better ships, stronger guns, and a greater need for economic growth, European powers descended upon West Africa with a fury. Ignoring traditional tribal boundaries, they sliced the region into colonies and took control of as many as they could defend. England took Ghana, Nigeria, and a few others. Cameroon was briefly German; Western Sahara was claimed by Spain. Most of the rest of West Africa was taken by the French.

Today, virtually all of these countries have gained their independence. Still, problems persist. Lumped together into states not of their own making and not of their choice, different cultures struggle for power and authority in many of the nations of West Africa. Countries such as Sierra Leone and the Ivory Coast have suffered especially brutal civil wars in recent years. Throughout much of the region, literacy rates remain low and child mortality levels high. Few Western nations, then or now, have done much to improve health care, education, or the economies of the countries of West Africa.

The Explorers' Legacy

In one sense, the problems of African countries today have little or nothing to do with the early explorers. Barth and Denham, Eanes and Lander—none of these men was involved in the Scramble for Africa. They did not make the political decisions that helped create the issues of today. In this view, it is unfair to blame Park, Cadamosto, Clapperton, and the rest for what happened after their expeditions came to an end.

Yet in another sense, the explorers are responsible for what happened after their time. Their work and courage in learning about the unknown lands to the south of Europe had the effect, whether intended or not, of making colonization possible. And the evidence is clear that many of the explorers, at least, would have approved. The early European traders, after all, had no moral dilemma in joining the slave trade; they saw the black Africans they met as not quite human.

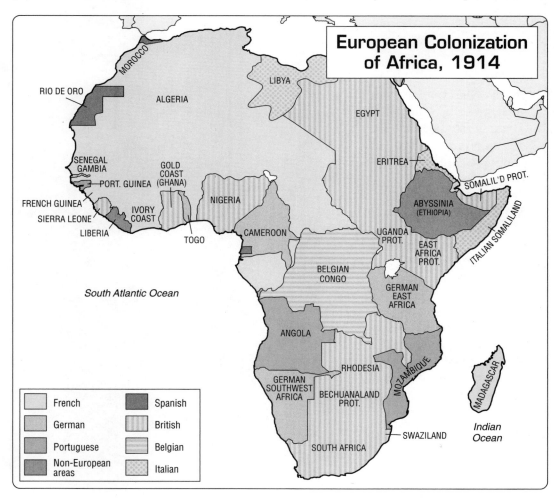

European Colonization of Africa, 1914

MOROCCO
RIO DE ORO
ALGERIA
LIBYA
EGYPT
SENEGAL
GAMBIA
PORT. GUINEA
GOLD COAST (GHANA)
ERITREA
SOMALIL'D PROT.
FRENCH GUINEA
SIERRA LEONE
IVORY COAST
NIGERIA
ABYSSINIA (ETHIOPIA)
LIBERIA
TOGO
CAMEROON
UGANDA PROT.
EAST AFRICA PROT.
ITALIAN SOMALILAND
BELGIAN CONGO
GERMAN EAST AFRICA
South Atlantic Ocean
ANGOLA
RHODESIA
MOZAMBIQUE
MADAGASCAR
GERMAN SOUTHWEST AFRICA
BECHUANALAND PROT.
Indian Ocean
SWAZILAND
SOUTH AFRICA

French
German
Portuguese
Non-European areas
Spanish
British
Belgian
Italian

Mary Kingsley

Among the most unusual and perceptive of later West African explorers was an English woman named Mary Kingsley. In 1893 she was struck with a sudden desire to visit the tropics, and after some research she chose to go to West Africa. Friends and acquaintances who had never even traveled to Africa immediately tried to dissuade Kingsley from undertaking the journey. One man who had actually visited the area also advised her against it. "When you have made up your mind to go to West Africa," this man told her, as quoted in Kingsley's book *Travels in West Africa,* "the very best thing you can do is to get it unmade again and go to Scotland instead."

Kingsley ignored all the advice she was given, and she was glad she did. She eventually made two trips, to Cameroon and Gabon. There she studied the cultures of several groups, most notably the Fang (or Fan) people of the Ogowe River region in present-day Gabon. The scientific-minded Kingsley also returned to England with specimens of fish, reptiles, and other West African animals. Along the way, Kingsley climbed the 13,500-foot-high Mount Cameroon, an active volcano, and had several narrow escapes with whirlpools, storms, and wild animals. "Awful turn up with crocodile about ten," she remarked in her diary at one point, quoted in her book. Kingsley became well known throughout England for her experiences in Africa; she was probably the most famous woman explorer of her time.

Kingsley studied the people, plants, and animals of West Africa, and she returned to England with a number of scientific specimens.

Later adventurers tended to perceive the people of West Africa as ignorant, dangerous, or both. The people of the region, in their eyes, were to be feared, hated, or pitied.

But the views of some explorers should not be taken to stand for all. A number of early travelers, including many Europeans, recognized the achievements of the cultures of West Africa. Park, Clapperton, and others appreciated the cities they visited and the thriving economies they encountered. And some explorers grew to appreciate individual West Africans or occasionally even entire societies. Park, for instance, had fond recollections of the black Africans who lived along his route to the interior. Barth, known for the interest he took in the lives of the people he visited, made several strong connections in the regions where he ventured. "We parted the best of friends," he wrote of one meeting with the son of a sultan, "greatly pleased with each other."[79]

The legacy of these adventurers, then, is mixed. On the one hand, there is no defending the slave trade, no defending the disdainful words and cruel actions of early travelers, no defending the greedy and uncaring policies toward West Africa that grew, in part, from the callous attitudes of the first European explorers. On the other hand, these travelers were creatures of their time, and there is no denying the courage, the resourcefulness, and the determination of those adventurers who undertook journeys of discovery to a continent about which they knew so little.

In the end, the deficiencies of the explorers should not take away from their achievements. The Europeans who ventured into West Africa were among the bravest adventurers the world has ever known. Not for nothing was West Africa considered, in Mary Kingsley's words, "the deadliest spot on Earth."[80] Clapperton, Park, Oudney, Richardson, Laing, Hornemann—an astonishing number of explorers of the region died while on their travels. Even those who survived suffered horribly from illness, thirst, and heat as they made their way through the fever-ridden swamps and across the bone-dry desert.

And yet, despite everything, these explorers kept going to West Africa and kept pushing on to learn whatever they could about the region. As Caillié and Laing put it, death was preferable to failure. That stubborn, sometimes fatal refusal to give in is at the heart of what it means to be an explorer. The Europeans who explored West Africa carried out their tasks admirably. Regardless of what else they may have done, their bravery, curiosity, and drive make their stories well worth remembering today.

Notes

Chapter 1: Early Tracks

1. Quoted in Richard Humble, *The Explorers: The Seafarers.* Alexandria, VA: Time-Life, 1978, p. 22.
2. Quoted in Humble, *The Explorers: The Seafarers,* p. 22.
3. Quoted in Robin Hallett, *The Penetration of Africa.* New York: Frederick A. Praeger, 1965, pp. 44–45.
4. Quoted in Hallett, *The Penetration of Africa,* p. 46.
5. Quoted in Hallett, *The Penetration of Africa,* p. 49.
6. Quoted in "World Maps of al-Idrisi," www.henry-davis.com/MAPS/EM webpages/219mono.html.
7. Quoted in "World Maps of al-Idrisi."
8. Quoted in Hallett, *The Penetration of Africa,* p. 53.
9. Ibn Battuta, *The Travels of Ibn Battuta,* vol. 4, translated by H.A.R. Gibb. London: Hakluyt Society, 1994, p. 946.
10. Ibn Battuta, *The Travels of Ibn Battuta,* vol. 4, p. 965.
11. Ibn Battuta, *The Travels of Ibn Battuta,* vol. 4, p. 948.

Chapter 2: The West African Coast

12. Quoted in Thomas Sterling, *Exploration of Africa.* New York: American Heritage, 1963, p. 31.
13. Gomes Eannes de Azurara, *The Chronicle of the Discovery and Conquest of Guinea,* vol. 1, New York: Burt Franklin, n.d., p. 27.
14. Azurara, *The Chronicle of the Discovery and Conquest of Guinea,* vol. 1, p. 28.
15. Christopher Hibbert, *Africa Explored.* New York: W.W. Norton, 1982, p. 16.
16. Azurara, *The Chronicle of the Discovery and Conquest of Guinea,* vol. 1, p. 31.
17. Azurara, *The Chronicle of the Discovery and Conquest of Guinea,* vol. 1, p. 33.
18. Quoted in G.R. Crone, ed., *The Voyages of Cadamosto.* London: Hakluyt Society, 1937, p. 3.
19. Quoted in Humble, *The Explorers: The Seafarers,* p. 28.
20. Quoted in Humble, *The Explorers: The Seafarers,* p. 30.
21. Azurara, *The Chronicle of the Discovery and Conquest of Guinea,* vol. 1, p. 36.
22. Quoted in Humble, *The Explorers: The Seafarers,* p. 30.
23. Ibn Battuta, *The Travels of Ibn Battuta,* vol. 4, p. 973.
24. Quoted in Humble, *The Explorers: The Seafarers,* p. 35.
25. Quoted in Crone, ed., *The Voyages of Cadamosto,* pp. 60–61.

26. Quoted in Crone, ed., *The Voyages of Cadamosto,* p. 16.
27. Quoted in Crone, ed., *The Voyages of Cadamosto,* p. 75.
28. Quoted in Hallett, *The Penetration of Africa,* pp. 60–61.
29. Quoted in Crone, ed., *The Voyages of Cadamosto,* pp. 32.

Chapter 3: The Search for the River Niger

30. Richard Jobson, *The Discovery of River Gambra,* edited by David P. Gamble and P.E.H. Hair. London: Hakluyt Society, 1999, p. 90.
31. Timothy Severin, *The African Adventure.* New York: Dutton, 1973, p. 53.
32. Quoted in Hallett, *The Penetration of Africa,* p. 127.
33. Quoted in Severin, *The African Adventure,* p. 63.
34. Quoted in C. Howard, ed., *West African Explorers.* London: Oxford University Press, 1951, pp. 66–67.
35. Quoted in John William Blake, ed., *Europeans in West Africa, 1450–1560,* vol. 2. London: Hakluyt Society, 1942, p. 424.
36. Quoted in Hallett, *The Penetration of Africa,* pp. 66–67.
37. Quoted in Blake, ed., *Europeans in West Africa, 1450–1560,* vol. 2, p. 422.
38. Quoted in Hallett, *The Penetration of Africa,* p. 127.
39. Quoted in Mungo Park, *Travels in the Interior Districts of Africa.* Durham, NC: Duke University Press, 2000, pp. 36–37.
40. Quoted in Park, *Travels in the Interior Districts of Africa,* pp. 67–68.
41. Quoted in Hallett, *The Penetration of Africa,* p. 231.
42. Quoted in Hallett, *The Penetration of Africa,* p. 233.
43. Quoted in Park, *Travels in the Interior Districts of Africa,* p. 171.
44. Quoted in Park, *Travels in the Interior Districts of Africa,* p. 180.
45. Quoted in Margery Perham and J. Simmons, *African Discovery.* 1943; reprint, London: Faber and Faber, 1963, p. 80.
46. Quoted in Park, *Travels in the Interior Districts of Africa,* p. 195.

Chapter 4: The Mouth of the Niger

47. Quoted in Fergus Fleming, *Barrow's Boys.* New York: Atlantic Monthly, 1998, p. 17.
48. Quoted in E.W. Bovill, ed., *Missions to the Niger,* vol. 1. Cambridge, England: Hakluyt Society, 1964, p. 95.
49. Quoted in Hibbert, *Africa Explored,* p. 82.
50. Quoted in E.W. Bovill, ed., *Missions to the Niger,* vol. 2. Cambridge, England: Hakluyt Society, 1966, p. 204.
51. Quoted in Howard, ed., *West African Explorers,* p. 174.
52. Quoted in Bovill, ed., *Missions to the Niger,* vol. 2, p. 244.
53. Quoted in Fleming, *Barrow's Boys,* p. 192.
54. Quoted in Hibbert, *Africa Explored,* p. 115.
55. Quoted in Perham and Simmons, *African Discovery,* p. 108.

56. Quoted in Howard, ed., *West African Explorers,* p. 300.
57. Quoted in Perham and Simmons, *African Discovery,* p. 97.
58. Quoted in Severin, *The African Adventure,* p. 130.
59. Quoted in Fleming, *Barrow's Boys,* p. 262.
60. Quoted in Hibbert, *Africa Explored,* p. 145.

Chapter 5: In Search of Timbuktu
61. Quoted in Fleming, *Barrow's Boys,* pp. 14–15.
62. Quoted in Bovill, ed., *Missions to the Niger,* vol. 1, p. 138.
63. Quoted in Fleming, *Barrow's Boys,* p. 203.
64. Quoted in Fleming, *Barrow's Boys,* p. 230.
65. Quoted in Bovill, ed., *Missions to the Niger,* vol. 1, p. 242.
66. Quoted in Bovill, ed., *Missions to the Niger,* vol. 1, p. 312.
67. Quoted in Hibbert, *Africa Explored,* p. 163.
68. Quoted in Hibbert, *Africa Explored,* p. 164.

69. Quoted in Piers Pennington, *The Great Explorers.* New York: Facts On File, 1979, p. 202.
70. Quoted in Howard, ed., *West African Explorers,* p. 342.
71. Quoted in Hibbert, *Africa Explored,* p. 169.
72. Quoted in Howard, ed., *West African Explorers,* p. 358.
73. Quoted in Howard, ed., *West African Explorers,* p. 371.
74. Quoted in Pennington, *The Great Explorers,* p. 203.
75. Quoted in Hibbert, *Africa Explored,* p. 177.
76. Quoted in Robert I. Rotberg, ed., *Africa and Its Explorers.* Cambridge, MA: Harvard University Press, 1970, p. 31.
77. Quoted in Hibbert, *Africa Explored,* p. 187.
78. Pennington, *The Great Explorers,* p. 207.

Conclusion: The Effects of Exploration
79. Quoted in Rotberg, ed., *Africa and Its Explorers,* pp. 33–34.
80. Mary H. Kingsley, *Travels in West Africa.* London: Macmillan, 1904, p.4.

Chronology

B.C.
ca. 600
Phoenicians circumnavigate Africa.

ca. 500
Hanno sails along West African coast.

ca. 450
Herodotus journeys into the northern
Sahara.

A.D.
42
Suetonius Paulinius crosses the Atlas
Mountains.

77
Pliny the Elder completes geographical treatises.

ca. 150
Ptolemy completes geographical work.

ca. 250
The writings of Solinus.

ca. 500s
Rise of Ghana Empire.

ca. 900s
Trade routes begin to cross the Sahara.

1154
Idrisi completes map and geographical
treatise.

ca. 1300s
Mali Empire at its height.

1352
Ibn Battuta visits Mali.

1415
Henry the Navigator conquers Ceuta.

1434
Gil Eanes rounds Cape Bojador.

1441
First African captives taken to Portugal.

1454–1456
Cadamosto's voyages along the West
African coast.

1457
Diogo Gomes travels up the Gambia
River.

1473
Fernando Po sails to the Bight of Biafra.

1482
Diogo Cão sails along entire West African
coast to the Congo River.

ca. 1500s
Songhai Empire is at its peak.

1621
Richard Jobson travels four hundred
miles up the Gambia River.

1788
African Association founded.

1789
Death of John Ledyard in Cairo.

1791

Death of Daniel Houghton on his way to the River Niger.

1795

Mungo Park leaves Gambia for the River Niger.

1796

Park is taken prisoner and escapes; reaches the Niger at Ségou.

1798–1801?

Friedrich Hornemann's journey toward the Niger ends in his death.

1805

Mungo Park reaches the Niger at Bamako.

1806

Park dies at Bussa.

1819

James Ritchie and George Lyon unsuccessfully try to cross the Sahara.

1822

Hugh Clapperton, Dixon Denham, and Walter Oudney leave Tripoli for Lake Chad.

1822

Gordon Laing explores Sierra Leone and locates the source of the Niger.

1823–1824

Clapperton, Denham, and Oudney explore the area around Kuka.

1826

Clapperton and Richard Lander reach the Niger at Bussa.

1826

Gordon Laing reaches Timbuktu and is killed on his way home.

1827

Death of Clapperton.

1828

René Caillié visits Timbuktu.

1830

Richard and John Lander journey down the Niger to its mouth.

1850

Heinrich Barth and James Richardson begin their expedition.

1851

Death of Richardson.

1853

Barth visits Timbuktu.

1855

Barth returns to Europe.

1893

Mary Kingsley's first expedition.

1894–1895

Kingsley's second expedition.

For Further Reading

Books

Don Brown, *Uncommon Traveler: Mary Kingsley in Africa*. Boston: Houghton Mifflin, 2000. A nicely illustrated biographical sketch of Mary Kingsley and her expeditions to West Africa.

Andrew K. Frank, *The Birth of Black America: The Age of Discovery and the Slave Trade*. New York: Chelsea House, 1996. Looks at the exploration of Africa by Europeans and its connection to the slave trade.

Aileen Gallagher, *Prince Henry the Navigator: Pioneer of Modern Exploration*. New York: Rosen Group, 2002. About Prince Henry, his life, and his role in the exploration of Africa.

Hazel Martell, *Exploring Africa*. New York: Peter Bedrick, 1997. A brief illustrated survey of outside exploration of Africa.

David Mountfield, *A History of African Exploration*. Northbrook, IL: Dornus, 1976. Information about African exploration in general; includes useful accounts of trips to West Africa.

James Rumford, *Traveling Man: The Journey of Ibn Battuta*. Boston: Houghton Mifflin, 2001. A well-illustrated and nicely poetic book about Ibn Battuta and his travels.

Web Sites

African History (http://africanhistory .about.com/od/explorers). General information about explorers of Africa, including links to time lines, primary sources, and other resources.

Kid Info (www.kidinfo.com/American _History/Explorers.html). Links to information on several Portuguese explorers.

The Mariners' Museum Age of Exploration Time Line (www.mariner .org/age/histexp.html). Links to various expeditions through the late 1700s.

Saharan Exploration (www.manntaylor .com/explore.html). Information about Saharan explorers and links to information about the lands and peoples of West Africa.

Works Consulted

Books

Gomes Eannes de Azurara, *The Chronicle of the Discovery and Conquest of Guinea.* 2 vols. New York: Burt Franklin, n.d. Translated by Charles Raymond Beazley and Edgar Prestage. Azurara's writings on the early Portuguese exploration of West Africa's coast, a work he completed in 1453.

John William Blake, ed., *Europeans in West Africa, 1450–1560.* 2 vols. London: Hakluyt Society, 1942. Documents relating to early European exploration of West Africa, together with commentary.

E.W. Bovill, ed., *Missions to the Niger.* Vol. 1. Cambridge, England: Hakluyt Society, 1964. Information and documents pertaining to the journeys of Friedrich Hornemann and Gordon Laing.

————, *Missions to the Niger.* Vol. 2. Cambridge, England: Hakluyt Society, 1966. Information and documents about the trek made across the Sahara by Dixon Denham, Hugh Clapperton, and Walter Oudney between 1822 and 1825.

Lester Brooks, *Civilizations of Ancient Africa.* New York: John Hawkins and Associates, 1971. Includes information on the Mali, Songhai, and other important empires of early West Africa.

G.R. Crone, ed., *The Voyages of Cadamosto.* London: Hakluyt Society, 1937. Cadamosto's own narrative of his journey to West Africa, along with other documents and commentary relating to his time and Portuguese seafaring in general.

Basil Davidson, *The African Slave Trade.* Boston: Little, Brown, 1961. A well-researched work on the slave trade with particular reference to the role played by Europeans.

Fergus Fleming, *Barrow's Boys.* New York: Atlantic Monthly, 1998. An engaging account of English exploration during the first half of the nineteenth century. A valuable source on the Clapperton-Denham expedition, along with information on Gordon Laing, Richard Lander, and others.

Robin Hallett, *The Penetration of Africa.* New York: Frederick A. Praeger, 1965. Expeditions to Africa through 1815. Especially thorough on the contributions of the people who visited Africa before the Portuguese. Also includes information on the first Europeans to travel into the West African interior.

Christopher Hibbert, *Africa Explored.* New York: W.W. Norton, 1982. A good general history of African exploration, with particular attention to the travels of the English in the West African interior from the time of Mungo Park.

C. Howard, ed., *West African Explorers*. London: Oxford University Press, 1951. A collection of primary-source documents written by European explorers of West Africa between 1600 and 1900. Includes the writings of Hugh Clapperton, Mungo Park, Heinrich Barth, and others.

Richard Humble, *The Explorers: The Seafarers*. Alexandria, VA: Time-Life, 1978. Includes important information about the early days of Portuguese navigation along the West African coast. Richly illustrated.

Ibn Battuta, *The Travels of Ibn Battuta*. Vol. 4. Translated by H.A.R. Gibb. London: Hakluyt Society, 1994. Ibn Battuta's last journeys are described in this book, including his trek to Mali.

Richard Jobson, *The Discovery of River Gambra*. 1623. Edited by David P. Gamble and P.E.H. Hair. Reprint, London: Hakluyt Society, 1999. Jobson's 1623 voyage up the Gambia River, which was also known at the time as the Gambra.

Mary H. Kingsley, *Travels in West Africa*. London: Macmillan, 1904. Kingsley made two voyages to Cameroon and other parts of the African coast. This book describes her experiences.

Charles David Ley, ed., *Portuguese Voyages*. London: Dutton, 1947. Excerpts from Portuguese mariners' accounts.

Includes some useful background information.

Mungo Park, *Travels in the Interior Districts of Africa*. Ed. Kate Ferguson Marsters. Durham, NC: Duke University Press, 2000. Park's own account of his first expedition.

Piers Pennington, *The Great Explorers*. New York: Facts On File, 1979. Explorers throughout history and their discoveries. Well illustrated with maps and other materials.

Margery Perham and J. Simmons, *African Discovery*. 1943. Reprint, London: Faber and Faber, 1963. Another anthology of letters and journal entries from various African explorers, including Mungo Park, Hugh Clapperton, and Richard Lander. The commentary is dated, but the documents are timeless.

Robert I. Rotberg, ed., *Africa and Its Explorers*. Cambridge, MA: Harvard University Press, 1970. A scholarly series of essays about various African explorers and their motives and impact on African societies. Includes a useful essay on Heinrich Barth.

Timothy Severin, *The African Adventure*. New York: Dutton, 1973. Another general history of African exploration. Severin devotes space to the early Portuguese as well as to the English.

Thomas Sterling, *Exploration of Africa*. New York: American Heritage, 1963. Well written and detailed. Includes information on Mungo Park, René Caillié, and the Portuguese explorers.

John W. Wright, ed., *The New York Times Almanac 2004*. New York: Penguin Reference, 2004. Facts and figures and some useful maps.

Internet Sources

Pekka Masonen, "Trans-Saharan Trade and the West African Discovery of the Mediterranean World," www.hf-fak.uib.no/institutter/smi/pai/Masonen.html.

University of South Carolina Libraries, "Exploring Africa," www.sc.edu/library/spcoll/sccoll/africa/africa4.html.

———, "Exploring Africa: Tennyson's 'Timbuctoo.'" www.sc.edu/library/spcoll/sccoll/africa/tenn.html.

"World Maps of Al-Idrisi," www.henry-davis.com/MAPS/EMwebpages/219mono.html.

Index

Picture Credits

About the Author

Stephen Currie is the creator of Lucent's Discovery and Exploration series. He also originated Lucent's Great Escapes series and has published many other books and articles. He lives with his family in New York State. He enjoys paddling on local rivers and lakes in a kayak neither as big nor as leaky as the canoes used by the Lander brothers on their journey down the Niger.